Asperger Solution

Kevin Foley

Seán Foley

Justine Connell

British Library Cataloguing In Publication Data
A Record of this Publication is available
from the British Library

ISBN 1846853982
978-1-84685-398-2

First Published 2006 by

Exposure Publishing, an imprint of Diggory Press,
Three Rivers, Minions, Liskeard, Cornwall, PL14 5LE, UK
WWW.DIGGORYPRESS.COM

Introduction

When my son, Sean was four years old a well meaning council official in a London borough told me not to worry about our application for a 'Statement of Educational Needs'. She said,

"Don't worry. You'll be fine. Your son is certain to get a 'statement' – he is well within the bottom 2%"

Thirteen years later, counting the proceeds from his genealogy stall in Milltown organic market (Co Kerry), he was pleased to inform me that he had

" ...Definitely exceeded [his] programming"

I had to agree.

Somebody with the foresight to have bought a few, once said that
'Lighting one candle is better than cursing the darkness'.
But, as anybody who has stumbled about in a power-cut knows -
finding a bloody candle in the bloody dark
means the bloody cursing comes first.

Being told your child has a disability plunges you into darkness.
Apparently we parents go through the phases of a grief cycle:
Shock; denial; anger; bargaining; depression; solution testing; acceptance.
We are entitled to the first 4 phases; we just can't get stuck there for too long and ideally we need to jump phase 5 and hit the ground running in phase 6.

If stage 7 means accepting things as they are – well to hell with that.
We have it in our power to change things for the better
– To disrupt the disruption to all our lives.
We can do that by changing the fundamentals
Or we can do that by changing the way we view the fundamentals.
Either way life gets better.

Getting back to the analogy …
We need to start looking for that bloody candle as
soon as we bloody well feel up to it.
At the risk of glorifying optimism –
I think the bloody candle is there to be found.

From raising my son and reading about other people's 'solutions',
I have come to appreciate just how much potential can be unlocked if we
empower ourselves and our children with the right skills and attitudes.
Our particular 'solution' involved decamping to the mountains sea and lakes of
Kerry and setting up 'home school'.
No better candle than a Kerry candle!
But every child and circumstance is unique – as will be every solution.

I am not an expert on anything – even my son. He keeps changing!
But I was a secondary school teacher for a quarter of a century.
Education can be an integral part of unlocking our child's potential but an
inappropriate 'educational' experience can blight their life and ours.

Given our children's idiosyncrasies an undue deference towards 'one-size-fits-
all' conventional schooling is unwarranted. I came to this conclusion under
duress - watching my son almost 'melt-down' under the pressure of
mainstream secondary schooling.
You would think I would have known better.

4

He's spent the last four years learning at home with me. I made the mistake of underestimating the risks inherent in letting other people dictate the pace, venue, timing, and content of his learning.

Teachers are by and large decent folk. They just don't want our autistic children in their mainstream schools. I was no different.

I must have encountered dozens of children with AS in my classrooms over a quarter of a century.

Minimising their stress was well down the list of my priorities.

Maximising their self-esteem was not my remit.

Mainstream teachers get press-ganged into being the main architects of autistic children's development.

But most of them don't want to do it - because they know they haven't got the time or the skills.

Forcing them to 'include' our children is a bit like teaching a pig to sing – it wastes precious time and annoys the pig.

Parents, meanwhile, too often expend all their energy battling a system that wasn't designed to cater for their children. Punching flies would be more productive.

What of the children themselves?

Some will do well in an academic sense
But there is a worst-case scenario.
One that I saw creeping up on my son when he was thirteen.

Studies indicate a high incidence of Depression amongst adolescents with AS
We also know that 'school' does inflict chronic stress on many adolescents with AS. (Irish Task Force on Autism)
Clinicians tell us that chronic stress can induce Depression.

Is it not logical to conclude from the above that mainstream schools can be risky places for autistic children?

Many teachers have gone under via the pressures.

Whither our children with their high propensity to experience anxiety and stress.

Depression can significantly impair the quality - and sometimes the quantity - of life for our children.

So - far from being the agent of inclusion 'school' can be the catalyst for a life-long exclusion.

Yet - if we *do* manage to avoid the onset of mental health problems the prognosis for autistic children who have developed language can be good. This means the premium to be reaped is simply **MASSIVE.**

I think we need to re-think the manner in which we educate our academically able autistic children.

By exposing them to full-time mainstream education we might be sailing far too fast and far close to the 'iceberg' of Depression. Because currently it's full steam ahead on the good ship INCLUSION - when what we really need is a lifeboat stocked up with flexibility and imagination.

By dint of personality, parental perseverance, and luck many children with AS may find a critical mass of supportive adults and peers in '*the system*'. This is fine – but should we really be trusting our child's mental health to the vagaries of staffing in a school. I don't think so. The risks *are* too great.

We need a more systematic approach.

We need to '**personalise**' their education to take full account of both their acute vulnerability and huge potential.

What follows is my take on what's wrong and what could be put right.

It may help some people arrive at 'solution testing' phase 6 faster than I did. .

Please allow me a few pages to curse the darkness.

I think it may be cathartic!

By way of an antidote to my imminent cursing - I'll start with the two most important insights I've gleaned from other people.

Talking of life with his autistic son, Nobel Prize winner Kenzaburo Oe reflected,

"I feel human beings can heal themselves; the will to be healed, and the power of recovery are very strong in us. That's the most important thing I've learnt in my life with my son.

I learnt the same thing from my son.

And then there's Rebecca Moyes – a teacher and the parent of an autistic child,

"Providing our children with the gift of self-esteem is always more effective than every dollar we spend on therapy and treatment to 'fix' Asperger Syndrome. "

If you need a mantra whilst you're finding your candle this takes some beating.

Notes

1. In the writing that follows I have been less than focused on gender balanced writing or current terminological debate. These things *do* matter ... but not as much as other things.

2. There may be some repetition of those things that I really want to get off my chest; I've had an autistic teenager and latterly his sheepdog puppy competing for my attention. Anyhow, saying some things more than once beats saying them less than once.

3. Analogies abound and there is at least one severely twisted metaphor - once a classroom teacher. This book isn't written for dispassionate literary critics. Inevitably *our* particular experiences will shape our perspectives and I am very aware that every child *is* unique – as are their circumstances. I have *tried not* to extrapolate or be didactic - but sitting on the fence would be a waste of good paper. Feel free to disagree

Cursing the darkness

Inclusion or Intrusion?

My in service training on Aspergers Syndrome (AS) consisted of a twilight session in a big school hall on a dark wet Wednesday in November. I'd been teaching solid for three days – my single 'free period' of the week so far having been lost to cover on the Tuesday .The INSET trainer in our twilight session was good but alas her students were not. She would have struggled had she been giving out the lottery numbers for that evening
…. then again maybe not.

At the time of the training I'd been a teacher for nearly twenty-three years. And a Dad for nearly thirteen years.

In common with most teachers I knew next to nothing about Aspergers Syndrome (AS). I'd already been teaching for four years before it was 'discovered'. Sean hadn't been diagnosed with AS at the time.

Parents think we know what we're doing when they send their autistic children into our mainstream schools. Most of us haven't a clue. And most of us don't want to have a clue. We just wish *they* would go somewhere else. Anywhere - as long as it's not our classroom; the job's difficult enough without the 'challenge' an autistic child presents in a class of 29 others.

Few mainstream schools relish the prospect of having a child with AS in their midst. It's a whole bunch of bother they could do without. In most cases what really happens when an autistic child walks through the door is more like *intrusion* than inclusion.

So ....not only do the majority of us teachers not know our AS from our elbow but we have little time or inclination to find out.
If you are a non-teacher you may think this all sounds very unprofessional. Can I suggest you try the job for a couple of terms before you condemn us.

Primary schools – especially in England - are losing an honourable rear-guard action to retain the holistic approach that used to make them *relatively* autism-friendly environments. Even reception class teachers have seen the home corner and sand table give way to the sensible business of achieving numeracy and literacy targets. Ireland is yet to be beset by this madness.

But primary schools are still relative havens of tranquillity for autistic children compared to the institution that they are subjected to next.

The pace in a typical secondary school is frenetic.
Beyond the 'safe haven' of the special needs room there isn't the time or the expertise to protect let alone nurture neurologically atypical children.

The excellent Irish Task Force on Autism sound a warning.

".... there is a huge gap between the primary and secondary provision and particularly those young people with AS who have the intellectual ability to cope with the secondary school curriculum but who do very badly there because the system there does not suit them <u>and they must run at very high stress levels.</u> Individual schools try to do their best but they do not understand what is involved."

There is a huge amount of cynicism in staff-rooms about the big push in these islands towards so-called '*inclusion*' of children with disabilities in mainstream schools.

In England there are plaudits for the LEA that gets the highest % 'included' - regardless of the actual nature of the disability or how this might play out at the chalk-face. For reasons best known to themselves, the plaudit givers deem it appropriate to use attendance at a mainstream school as a proxy for 'inclusion'.

The cynicism is based on the perception that the vast sums of money saved by *not* sending children to 'special' schools never fully makes its way back to recipient mainstream schools.

In fact special needs teachers in mainstream schools spend half their time jumping through bureaucratic hoops to get much needed extra help for these children.

So what *is* happening is simple placement *not* inclusion.

Genuine inclusion is about moulding the institution around the individual. This doesn't happen. In fact, given the complexity of their needs, it can't happen. It's disingenuous - and even dangerous - to pretend it does.

Don't blame the teachers. They are merely focused on the core function of the school as determined by their 'betters'. Schools are set the task of processing children through a prescribed curriculum The holy grail of all the blood sweat and tears: Examinations. Lots of them. It's what society expects; a rite of passage inflicted by each generation of adults on each generation of children. So it's what teachers do.

Unlike some children on the autistic spectrum, our children with AS *have* developed language; this being the main difference between 'aspies' and children with so-called *classic* autism.

The prognosis can ultimately be 'good' for autistic people who have language. It may take time for the 'penny to drop' but drop it often does

So - to emphasise a key point - there is a simply **massive premium** to be gained from helping children to avoid the chronic stress that can bring on mental health issues. People with AS can, given time, teach themselves to cope; people with AS *and* mental health problems will never cope.

This begs the question:

How can mainstream Schools be lauded as agents of *inclusion* if they themselves can be a catalyst for mental health problems and ultimately *exclusion?*

"**The good news is he's bright, the bad news is he's bright.**"
(Irish Task Force on Autism)

It's too simplistic to refer to people with Aspergers Syndrome as 'mildly autistic' or having a 'mild' disability. Their intelligence quotient gradually strips them of the autistic bubble that they may have had when they were younger. Increasing self-awareness enables them to feel more deeply the pain of being 'different'. There's absolutely nothing mild about being the inept outsider – especially when you are a teenager.
The gap between what you look as though you *should* be able to do and what you *can* do matters. It can't be easy - disappointing people all the time. ...

It's put well in the following phrase,

'That it is the mildness of the handicap in AS that makes its emotional and social impact so severe.' (Tatam 2000)

For a teenager the pain of being *nearly* 'normal' is huge; the damage done possibly irreparable. Craving friendship yet experiencing ridicule and derision has to be the source of deep long lasting hurt. A friendless teenager who is ostracised and isolated *must* sometimes wish that they did not have this burning desire to 'fit in' – like a moth to a flame. The confusion and indignation of getting 'it' wrong all the time can - if we let it - make for a miserable existence.

If they progress along the spectrum there is merely a re-allocation of pain between the stake-holders: We get happier; they can get sadder.
Every positive movement in cognitive functioning brings with it an enhanced ability to compare oneself to gregarious and socially successful peers.

And being *nearly normal* also keeps you 'in bounds' for being tormented by peers. People in wheelchairs or people who have obvious physical indicators of disability will, by contrast, usually be 'out of bounds' for all but the nastiest of bullies. Not so for people with the 'hidden' disability of AS.

Calls for *'Inclusion for all'* i.e. mainstream placements, take no account of the varying propensity of different disabilities to be targets for bullying.
Given the possible implications of bullying this is a major oversight.
We can rectify this oversight.

Not every 'aspie' is a 'Rainman' ...or even a Forest Gump

A minority (5-10%) of autistic people have special skills a la 'Rainman'. These can be splinter skills such as my son knowing everything about Coronation Street from 1961-2006. Or prodigious skills such playing a piano concerto perfectly after just one listening.

What everybody on the spectrum does have in common is a set of deficits and/or delays. Their different neurology interferes with: their ability to process and prioritise information from their senses efficiently; their ability to respond with appropriate actions and words that others might see as 'normal'; their ability to empathise with the thoughts and feelings of others; their ability to understand the rules of all the 'games' we play with each other – whether the game involves facial expressions or words or balls; their ability to take the initiative in novel situations using related knowledge from past experiences ; their fine and gross motor skills .

In this last respect there is a big overlap with Dyspraxia.
Indeed many children with AS/HFA have had an earlier diagnosis of Dyspraxia. These deficits and delays make interaction with other people either impossible or difficult and painful. If they develop speech it still doesn't mean they know how to use it to play with other children and make friends. Their innocence makes it even harder to be a parent watching their failures unfold. .

Autism makes all the rites of passage more difficult to achieve. School will be a frustrating obstacle course. Autism will dramatically reduce the opportunity to find and keep well-paid work. It will therefore reduce disposable lifetime income. It will reduce the opportunity for successful interaction with the opposite sex and marriage and children. It will reduce the probability of independent living. Most worryingly it increases the chance of suffering from a mental illness: Suicide is correspondingly a bigger risk.

This facet of the syndrome is the most frightening.

So we have to ensure that autistic children do not enter adolescence with a disability and exit it with both a disability and mental health problems.

Autism is not an illness. We have to stop it resulting in one.

Experts my bottom

Not the GP who sends you home with a pat on the head. Not the teacher who regales you with your child's limitations at a parents evening.

Not the consultant who misdiagnoses or charges 1000 euro for a corroborative diagnosis. (be wary of talking to internationally renowned experts after conferences)

Not the educational psychologist who routinely 'includes' autistic children in mainstream secondary schools.

Not the Psychiatrist who ignores the diagnosis of autism and advocates anti-psychotic drugs.

Not the policeman who sections your child once the anti-psychotic drugs produce psychotic episodes.

None of these people are experts and – crucially – they *care* a lot less than you do. The frightening thing that does gradually dawn on you is that you, as a parent, are the nearest thing to an expert on this planet. And you have the job for life.

It is likely that getting that diagnosis and acting on it from an informed standpoint will be the biggest determinant of your child's quality of life.

The diagnostic tools exist now; if it walks like a duck and it quacks like a duck. …it's a bloody duck!!

Recent research indicates suspicion of autism is very rarely misplaced.

And if *somebody doesn't* identify it as a 'duck 'early enough, we might end up with a dead duck!

A diagnosis at an average age of 11 is not good enough.

"In addition to their core condition, they frequently suffer from affective disorders such as depression. Suicide attempts are not unusual for this group particularly during the teenage years. Many children/adolescents are deeply troubled by their social ineptitude, their lack of social acceptance by peers and their isolation and rejection."
(Irish Task Force on Autism)

I still can't believe how **placid** the whole bloody system seems to be in the face of this possible outcome. **WAKE UP SYSTEM!**

There is no safety net for teenagers in meltdown

Normal autistic responses to stressors can be misinterpreted as psychotic episodes. In years gone by many people displaying autistic responses to stressors would have found themselves incarcerated in asylums.

This still happens today, *even* when a diagnosis of autism has already been made.

In these circumstances the administration of anti-psychotic drugs to control behaviour is likely to prove ineffective.

Using an anti-psychotic drug to control environmentally induced behaviour is nothing short of abuse. It should never be the first option. Removing the stressors and putting coping strategies in place *may* be more time-consuming but it is much less dangerous, much more effective, and much cheaper.

Drugs should never be a cop out for busy parents and clinicians; especially since the procedure to combat psychosis seems to be a hit and miss operation; **'if one drug doesn't work try the next one'.**

This appalling scenario is a reality for some autistic people who find themselves subjected to a chemical cosh.

Health authorities in the US have ruled that anti-depressants used by children must carry a 'black box warning to show that they carry an *increased* risk of suicide in some patients.

After months reviewing the international data on the drugs, known as SSRIs (selective serotonin reuptake inhibitors), the UK's drugs regulator, the Medicines and Healthcare Products Regulatory Agency, has concluded that GPs are prescribing far too many pills for people who do **not** have a serious clinical condition.

There was a time when I would have been deferential to those who know twice as much as me about neurons and brain chemistry. But since I only know 1% of what needs to be known they are, in truth, not that much further down the road: If they *were* we would not have trial and error administration of anti-depressant drugs.

Some people in the system seem to a bit too cavalier with other people's brain chemistry.

It's vital we help people with AS stay out of the mental health system.

In Ireland the situation is if anything worse than in the UK.

This was spelt out in **The Irish Examiner** – 31/5/04 – by Cormac O'Keeffe and Michael O'Farrell. They wrote,

In the latest report by the Inspector of Mental Hospitals...there [is] a virtual absence of in-patient residential care for children and adolescents...since 1998 nearly 3,000 – mostly young people – have committed suicide...rather than allocating funds to suicide research and prevention programmes ...the symptoms of a condition that can lead to suicide are treated by anti-depressants and sedatives... if proper psychiatric services were provided for young people between the ages of 11 and 15 when warning signs of subsequent illness tend to emerge it could avert major problems later and ease the burden of mental illness on the health services. In 2003 the country spent 50 million euro on anti-depressants.

If society doesn't have a safety net shouldn't we be taking less risks with the mental health of autistic children. **Prevention is the only show in town**

Si ma tante avait ballons elle serait mon oncle.

If *only* Hans Asperger had written up his thoughts about his 'eccentric boys ' in English. If he had done that in the 1940's, clinicians and educators in these islands would have had a forty year head start in familiarising themselves with it.

It would probably have meant an accurate diagnosis for my son nine years before it finally arrived.

Autism interferes with all the early skills that parents work on with their children: talking, walking, toileting, dressing, running, eating, drawing. Making them so much more difficult to impart.

Meanwhile all the other kids are hitting the milestones like clockwork and it's time to play a stressful game of catch-up. The battle to be 'normal' is peppered with setbacks that other parents aren't having.

Emotional responses that seem to be coming from nowhere. If you don't know a child is hypersensitive to touch or loud noises you can't work out *why* he is screaming or doesn't want to sit on your knee for more than one second. It would really help to have the compass pointing in a specific direction at this frustrating time.

Special schools for AS *do* exist.

It's important for those in the know to tell those who are **not** in the know what they need to know.

Parents should be given information on the various options that exist at secondary level for their child – irrespective of the relative cost of the provision Not to do so is unprofessional.

Decisions made without accurate information are more likely to be poor ones. 24% of parents do **not** think they understood the educational options before choosing a place for their child; 21% found the information they were able to obtain inadequate and 40 % found choosing a school hard; 9 % of parents *still* feel they do not know what sort of education their child should be getting (19 % in Scotland) **from Inclusion and Autism: Is it working?** by Barnard Prior and Potter NAS.

And this is not taking the 'unknown unknowns' into accounts! Most parents are not in a position to know what's available and what's best. Unfortunately they place their trust in people who don't know either.

In this context, it is interesting to note the U-turn recently performed by Baroness Warnock.

She who got the 'inclusion' bandwagon rolling 25 years ago now cites the pressure to *'include'* as the cause of

".. confusion of which children are the casualties."

You have to respect people who change their minds in the light of experience But there will have been many casualties in the interim.

That the system is chaotic is evidenced by the resignation of NHS neuropsychologist Janis Newcomen. (Observer 30/7/06). She is heading back to the USA on the Queen Mary 2 leaving behind her diagnostic work in the field of autism and..

"... a corrupt and dysfunctional system that is dishonest in its treatment and management of children with special needs"

Her professional opinion is that given the paucity of funding for 'inclusion' 3 out of 4 of the autistic children she has seen would have been better served outside the mainstream.

(If 3 out of 4 operate at the AS end of the spectrum this means she believes the majority with AS are currently ill-served by 'inclusion')

Revealingly she adds,

"We are told the goal is 'inclusion' and the goal is not to statement because that needs extra money.we cannot say the child would benefit from a special school.

At the very least parents should be given information about the specialist education providers that do exist.

There was no *golden* age for being different but....

At a time when anything that wasn't nailed down was being privatised, the one thing to get nationalised in the UK of the 1980's was ... children.

As the nations 'crown jewels' were being *liberated* our crown jewels were being conscripted to the service of the State.

Micro-management of teacher and taught arrived via The National Curriculum, Ofsted and League Tables.

The fear Ofsted engenders in schools has to be experienced to be believed; many a good teacher has succumbed to it.

This unholy trinity gradually poisoned the environment for children who need a less pressurised learning environment.

I once set up a mini-enterprise for a group of fairly disaffected 14yr olds. One of the group had a real passion for garden gnomes. We raised some cash by selling shares, bought some moulds, and made and sold them at the school fete The exercise was cross-curricular, good fun and very educational – they had loads of problems to solve along the way. I remember the 'managing director' legging it down the fields after the 'purchasing manager'- intent on doing him damage 'cos he thought some funds had gone on fags not gnomes.

I wouldn't dare ask other departments to give up some of their test/exam tuition time nowadays for something as frivolous as this. Indeed it might be *illegal.* Under the 2002 Education Act, the much missed Professor Ted Wragg

RIP pointed out, (The Guardian 21/12/04) schools have to write to the Minister if they want to 'innovate'.

As older staff will tell you, the flexibility and *soul* has gone out of the curriculum. There is no incentive to do something that can't be tick boxed, accredited and/or used to get threshold pay. As long as the criterion for success is so narrow, and as long as fear is deemed to be the most effective motivator of teachers, you can forget about *Inclusion.*

Most teachers are subject teachers before they are anything else. The entire ethos of many schools has been condensed into a drive to move up the exam league table. And this is unsurprisingly making very few in the school community happier.

"The route people take to adulthood has become much more difficult with the pressure on for qualifications."
– John Coleman, director of the trust for the study of adolescence.

The mental health of teenagers in general has sharply declined in the last 25 years. Research conducted by academics in London and Manchester (Time Trends in Adolescent Mental Health 1974-99: Journal of Child Psychology and Psychiatry Nov. 04)) shows the rate of emotional problems such as anxiety and depression to have increased by 70% from 1974 to 1999.
In the longer term the teams find these problems to be good predictors of the propensity to be sacked, dependency on benefits, health problems and homelessness.

We are literally driving children mad.

In the 1970's when I started teaching, less bookish children could leave school at 16 to go into craft and technician apprenticeships. Some left earlier to find work in the community or with family. They could earn money and feel they had a stake in society. And respect. There was light at the end of a relatively short tunnel because relative failure alongside more academic peers was less prolonged. They behaved well (most of the time) because they needed references at the age of 16.

The focus today in the UK is achieving some arbitrary target of 50% going to University. The message is very much that *not* going to 'Uni' constitutes **failure** for the individual. Why don't we just give out white feathers to those who don't make the cut. Don't they know their country needs them – although evidently not as apprentice plumbers or chippies!

To the extent better qualifications deliver higher incomes it could be agued that the interests of the individual coincide with the apparent interests of the nation. (Though this is **not** true for the 38% of graduates who end up in employment that does not require a third level qualification.)   Forcing or bribing less academic teenagers to stay in school and deliver written work at a pace and on a scale that ill suits them makes no sense. They know it – that's why so many truant.

In some schools 80% of children will *not* get the magic 5 A-C's yet the diet remains stubbornly inflexible. Look no further for some of the main reasons behind their disruption and disaffection.   Many secondary schools in England are fairly unhappy places for teacher and taught. Tony Blair called teachers in inner-city schools 'saints and heroes a couple of years back…and we all know what happens to saints and heroes.
STOP PRESS: most of these *saints and heroes* have just been threatened with the sack if their individual %s don't stack up and stay up!

Teachers *would* have more time for … children
- if it wasn't for all the outside interference from politicians.
Initiative follows initiative and leaves no room for. …initiative.
Teachers cannot think 'outside the box' because they are so busy bloody ticking 'em.

How can we expect the most vulnerable children to thrive in such institutions. *And* how exactly do they learn social skills merely via their physical presence in this kind of community.

Those Schools up the *top* end of the league tables intend staying there by strict focus on things that can be measured. Children with AS are an annoying distraction from these objectives. The situation in Ireland is better – but there is growing pressure to anglicise the system.

There are a whole range of coping skills that are allocated very little time in a conventional secondary school curriculum.

There is little *intrinsic* value or joy in the courses taken in secondary schools. Most are treated as a means to a narrow end.
Even core skills such as numeracy and literacy have been undermined by teaching which is focused purely on getting teenagers through exams Universities have to spend half their time teaching basic numeracy and literacy – yet A level results keep getting better and better!
The politicisation of the system has driven out integrity; the exam emperor has no clothes.

All the other *extra* skills that adolescents with AS need to be taught are nowhere to be seen. Some people have already noticed this deficiency,

"...many adults with AS may be 'well educated' but are unable to manage cooking or even seek appropriate help if they have a physical medical condition."
Angela Browning MP 23/10/01 in House of Commons.

Of course these people are **not** actually '*well educated*'; they have merely been processed as exam fodder.
Mainstream schools are **not** set up to deal with young autistic people.

You might as well ask a car factory producing saloons to do the odd sports car now and again.

If an autistic person reaches the age of 21 with paper qualifications but unable to cope with 'life' then the adults who have overseen that process have failed to do their job properly.

Those of us charged with their care have a duty to help them acquire life enriching skills and attitudes. And this is a huge task; neuro-typicals can extrapolate easily from previous experience and apply learnt skills to new situations. Not so with most autistic people; meaning appropriate responses and actions take much longer to put in place.

Teaching these skills is time consuming and beyond the remit of a conventional school placement.

But if these skills are **not** taught then the phrase **Individual Education Plan (IEP)** is virtually meaningless.

Too often IEP's consist *only* of ways of plugging identified gaps in the child's understanding of concepts that will appear in some future exam, as opposed to the delivery of anything like a holistic package.

I have yet to see one that stressed the need to avoid stress!

The skills our children need to learn are as diverse as social skills, relaxation techniques, self-sufficiency skills leisure skills, looking after animal skills, kitchen skills, hoover skills; answering the door to hawker skills, dealing with sexual feeling ; dealing with not being able to find a girl/boyfriend skills, etc Coping with the routines of daily life is a very important determinant of quality of life – even more significant than a person's income level.

Moreover, as important as the *actual* success from having life skills, is the person's *perception* of their efficacy. Two different people experiencing the same things can interpret the events very differently. I have to work really hard to help my son to see the glass as half-full. I don't want other adults undermining that work.   Preparing these children for exams should be fitted in around the teaching of coping skills. Not the other way around.

At some point we need to ask the question –

'What is the problem to which a mainstream secondary school is the answer'?

Mainstream secondary schools are provided free at the point of consumption. This is the case because education is, what economists call, a 'merit good ' Consuming education has private benefits for the student, but also huge 'external' benefits' i.e. *other* people *also* benefit from the fact that the student can read, write, and compute.

The main external benefit is that the student becomes part of an educated workforce. As trading nations Ireland and Britain need to remain competitive in order to maintain and continually improve material living standards.

Politicians get re-elected or dumped primarily on pocket-book issues. And since they get to make the rules, we naturally have an education system that serves the needs of the economy not the individual.

In terms of the current levels of inward investment into the UK and Ireland the value added to our children by the 'system' is good enough: Give or take the odd teacher suicide, and an epidemic of adolescent self-harm, the human capital being produced seems to validate the education systems in these islands.

Given the importance of this outcome it is easy to see why UK politicians in particular have chosen to micro-manage the system.

The rigidity this has conferred on schools has unfortunately made them less welcoming and useful to our *non-standard* inputs.

The latest wheezes in England are to use data to identify and sack 'bad' teachers and close down failing schools within one year. Teachers will be even *less* inclined to have an autistic child in their class once these witch-hunts are in place.

To isolate the real driving force in the system, watch what happens next time there are changes in the school curriculum or a proposal to alter examinations. The CBI is always invited to comment first, then Headteachers, then parents, then possibly classroom teachers – nobody asks the kids. What does that tell you about the priorities in the system?

This is **not** a system that has the holistic education of *anybody*, let alone autistic children, as its core function. It just isn't good enough to pose the question ' **can autistic children cope in a mainstream school** *?*
The question has to be '**will autistic children derive the most benefit from being in a mainstream school?**

The jury isn't so much 'out' – it hasn't been formed yet

The cost of being autistic.

The Irish taxpayer will be giving five million euro to the Autism Genome Project.. The Project is seeking to identify the genes responsible for hereditary autism. The fact that so many countries are willing to cough up so much money is indicative of the financial implications of autism. In recognition of this, there *are* separate institutions for autistic children who have additional and significant intellectual impairments. (Classic Autism). These institutions allow mainstream schools to operate more efficiently. The downside for the state is that Special schools are expensive to operate; but if you want to close them down and save money, you need to find an *educational* pretext *for* doing so i.e. Inclusion. There are also units operating within mainstream schools that seek to re-integrate more academically able autistic children into a traditional curriculum. The main problem I have with such units is the criteria used for success – it seems, in general, to be 'how closely the child can ape the experience of their non-autistic peers '. The intervention can therefore have more to do with the school's needs than the child's needs.

But at least with these units, autistic children have somebody in the school who is 'in their corner'. However, *even* with such genuine and laudable attempts to help autistic children, the motivation of those who hold the purse strings is suspect.

In running such a unit in Sheffield, Matthew Hemondshalgh and Christine Breakey use their book **Access and Inclusion for children with Autistic Spectrum Disorders,** to confide their concerns,
"On occasions their (Sheffield LEA) overriding aim appeared to be a reduction in costs...." They go on to outline the key numbers,
"The typical cost of provision outside Sheffield that caters for pupils with ASD is approximately £40,000 (which would be much higher if there were a residential element to the provision) Our cost per student is less than £9000 per annum...." That 'saving' of £31,000 will, I believe, always undermine the credibility of some of those who are pushing an 'Inclusion' agenda. In April 2000 Professor Martin Knapp and Krister Jarbink of the Centre for the Economics of Mental Health estimated...

" The annual total cost of autistic disorder in the UK is at least £1 Billion. The greatest costs are for living support (70%) and day activities (14%) ...education (7%)."

Most tellingly they concluded that ...
"Evidence suggests that even moderate increases in educational provision could potentially result in savings in later living costs. The average additional lifetime cost for people with high-functioning autism is £784,785. ...schooling, residential care/living support, sheltered employment costs, hospital care, medication, lost productivity, loss of parental earnings, social services, respite care, ...potentially great savings could be achieved by interventions that increase the possibility of independent living.

We arrange the education of large numbers of children by small numbers of adults for one reason ... it's cheaper! Only in the case of children with AS ... it isn't!

The cost-effectiveness is totally undermined if a child's potential is damaged by the process; *then* it becomes a *very* expensive option.

Given the above numbers, trying to process autistic adolescents on the cheap obviously makes no sense whatsoever – even on the narrowest of financial grounds. But if you are a budget holder in a cash-strapped education authority your brief is purely a short-term one; the cheapest placement has to be the most attractive to you. The future is somebody else's problem.

As every student of economics knows, inefficient decisions are made when *Consumer Ignorance* exists. Education, like health, is a product where the consumer is likely to be unaware of all the costs and benefits. There is a reliance on others – professionals - to act ethically and advise on the best 'treatment' available. If we go to a doctor with a pain in the leg we need to be sure that he will not recommend amputation just because there is a bigger profit to be made. If we take advice about school placement from professionals we would hope it would be given irrespective of budgetary considerations. As was indicated above by Dr Newcomen, that hope is usually a forlorn one - even though failure to invest in autistic children is clearly a false economy.

Fair play to Maria Hutchings, mother to 10 year old John, who took Tony Blair to task on live TV (The Wright Stuff 16/2/05) for the impending closure of John's special school. We cannot just sit back and watch politicians blather and bureaucrat's bluster whilst funding for autistic children is cut.

Children are the only resource to have been nationalised in the last thirty years. Perhaps it's time that parents privatised them again. Special schools are being closed down in the UK (200 in the decade 1992-02) at the same time as *choice* is being trumpeted as the catalyst for improvement. Is this not blatant discrimination against families with children who have disabilities?

The *Special Schools Protection League* believe that the inclusion agenda has been hijacked by education authorities intent on saving money: LEA's direct children away from special schools; their rolls fall to the point where they are not viable; they close; the site is sold off.

In the meantime mainstream schools are acquiring *specialist* status in technology, or sports, or languages etc (Please don't look *too* closely for big differences once the paint is dry on the new gate sign and the cash is in the coffers.) Most headteachers have had to tie up huge amounts of management time bidding for this money; but it's just another hoop the politicians have dreamt up for teachers to jump through.
Back in the classroom, it all looks pretty much the same.

All in all then - nomenclature apart - what we have is a **diminution** of choice for the parents of autistic children: Less schools specializing in autism and more schools 'specializing' in form filling.

In the TES 16/10/04 Mary Dhonau, Parent Governor of Thorton House special school, Worcester is bemused by the trend ...

"I have to ask why 'inclusion' has to take place within a mainstream school?

I know of no other school that 'includes' children more than Thorton House School does. To my great sorrow this school unfortunately is closing because of the governments inclusion agenda...the whole school celebrates every achievement no matter how small...yesterday my son dressed up as a postman and delivered the post to every classroom in the school." If it feels like you are trying to nail jelly to the ceiling, there should come a point where you ask yourself *WHY* you want the jelly on the ceiling in the first place!

The daily diet of stress and anxiety experienced by many autistic children in mainstream secondary schools means we should find **very** good reasons for keeping them there. Especially since so much energy goes into achieving, what is after all, only an *intermediate* objective.

One analogy which tries to explain the autistic view of the world concerns a flashlight. When shone on a wall we, neuro-typicals, supposedly see the *entirety* of the wall lit up. An autistic person will typically focus on a small section of the wall, to the exclusion of the surrounding area.

This is supposed to exhibit *their* inability to see the 'big picture'; *their* narrow perspective.

But, ironically, this tunnel vision is exactly what many of us display when it comes to deciding an appropriate education for our autistic children.

We miss the big picture because we too are blinkered; we *know* that the mainstream has a very narrow agenda but we stick with it.

Meanwhile the years roll by and then.... one day we wake up and we have a young person with exam certificates and no idea how to cope with *life*.

Placement differs from integration and integration differs from inclusion.

Inclusion is **such** an attractive notion. To be 'included' touches a nerve with our sense of fair play. We all yearn to be *included,* so it's hardly surprising that this is our most heartfelt desire for our children: For them to be accepted - for them to have friends. And yet the reality of what passes for inclusion at chalk-face level falls well short of this laudable objective. Life in a mainstream secondary school for an autistic child can be brutal torrid and traumatic. It is worth getting a few definitions straight: Inclusion in an institution occurs when the institution adapts itself to fit in with the needs of the individual: **"Inclusive education is a process involving the restructuring of the curriculum and classroom organisation" Inclusion and Autism: Is it working? by Barnard Prior and Potter NAS 2000.**

Of course, mainstream Schools don't do this. They can't be expected to. Real 'inclusion' does not happen. It can't happen.

What we get is **quasi-inclusion** which looks fine and dandy from a distance (as close as most politicians and bureaucrats usually get)

Integration **in an institution occurs when an individual is given help to cope with the demands of that institution.**
Given the limited time and expertise available for teaching social and life skills in the school day, integration doesn't really happen that much either - especially in secondary school. The support is mostly so the child can follow the academic programme – this isn't integration.

Consequently, **by definition**, we can't really talk about children with autism being '*included'* **or** even *integrated'* in mainstream schools. All that is effectively happening to most autistic children is a *placement* - with daily 'fire fighting' for the next five years to keep them in the building. 50% don't make it through the obstacle course.

This is not to belittle the sterling efforts of those few people who try to make life more tolerable for autistic adolescents. But as Prior and Potter go on to emphasise,

"Schools need to buy in wholesale to 'Inclusion' if it is to work. Inclusion cannot rely on the interest commitment and enthusiasm of one or two individuals. Without a shift in the whole organisation's attitude and approach it will fail children with autism and Aspergers Syndrome."

Given *real* 'inclusion' involves such wholesale upheavals to curriculum, classroom organisation, and the actual ethos of a school, we need to acknowledge that *inclusion* in a mainstream school is **not** a realistic objective.

But the notion that *inclusion* actually *happens* in schools is disingenuously used to justify the placement of vulnerable children in largely unmodified and stressful environments.

Placement in a mainstream secondary school is increasingly the norm for high functioning autistic children.

But placement in a mainstream school should be a means to an end not an objective to be achieved for its own sake, to be retained at all costs.

As **Rebecca A Moyes** points out in her book **'Incorporating Social Goals in the Classroom'.**

".. signing a child up for an inclusive placement without the supports he/she needs is like sealing a child's failure in regular education...inclusion is only beneficial if the child is profiting from it. Parents and educators need to look closely at the word 'profit' and weigh the disadvantages with the advantages...advocates for inclusion need to consider whether the idea of full inclusion is worth the trade-off of the student's mental health. "

In my experience the levels of support that many autistic children need are not being provided in the mainstream.

They are neither being included or integrated.

Mainstream secondary schools are 'institutionally exclusive'

"He shouldn't be here." is a common enough complaint in staffrooms. Because teachers do not generally appreciate the difference between wilfully bad behaviour and an emotional outburst brought on by an atypical neurology under stress.

The scale of the task facing the teacher being that much greater because no two autistic children will present with the same 'symptoms'.

'There is no exact recipe for classroom approaches that can be provided for every youngster with Asperger Syndrome' – aspire guidance for teachers' booklet.

32

What that means is that every subject teacher will have to get to know how a particular child with autism responds to him/her, their unique classroom environment, the other children in the teaching group, homework, practicals, noises, smells and so on.

Very little of what was learnt with a previous autistic student can simply be re-applied.

So teachers need more than just *general* training about AS.

Every child with AS has a **unique** endowment of strengths and challenges. Insight into AS in general does not translate into useful strategies for a particular individual.

If, in the INSET I had, I **had** been given strategies to use with the AS child in **my** class the following morning I would have listened **very** carefully.

It would have been in my interest to do so; people learn best when they can identify something in it for them.

Far better this nitty-gritty guidance, than another set of handouts, or some glitzy PowerPoint presentation from an 'expert' on AS.

The parent of the individual child is the expert you need to talk to.

In order to be of *real* use teachers need information specific to an individual child; strategies that simultaneously helps the child *and* makes life easier for the teacher.

Until autistic children and their teachers have the type of focused support they need - and the funding to go with it - children with AS will be generally unwelcome in mainstream schools. Anybody who tells you otherwise isn't a classroom teacher.

Cross-phase sometimes means crossed wires too

No matter how much paper changes hands between primary and secondary school, the latter will typically still - at least in the early stages - be fairly oblivious to the needs of the child.

Cross-phase links - between primary and secondary - are a bit of a Cinderella activity.

Schools go through the motions but the information gleaned rarely makes it through to the chalk-face in the secondary school.

If the information *does* make it through - pressure in the system means it is often effectively ignored by the average classroom teacher. September is a very busy time.

Only when problems actually arise in the secondary school will lessons about the child be re-learnt.

Stretching the lines of communication between two schools might seem straightforward to the outsider. In reality primary schools and secondary schools are like chalk and cheese. Both sets of professionals view each other with a certain awe.

Neither knows what the other does or how the other does it – in all senses! And there is neither time nor sufficient interest to find out.

Once again the child is likely to be badly served due to levels of ignorance. There can be an in-built bias towards overestimation of the child's ability to deal with secondary school. And an underestimation of the stressors that the child will face in moving through adolescence in a much more demanding environment. Teachers in primary school know and care for the child as he is, where he is. Whilst they are not oblivious to the challenges ahead for him, the sheer scale of the problems will often *not* be part of their professional experience.

So, the information available to make good decisions in that life-determining placement meeting is deficient.

It could hardly be otherwise.

If I were in that room, as a secondary school liaison teacher, with the experience I now have, I would let the parents know just how difficult and dangerous a mainstream secondary school *might* be for their child. If I were in that room, I would also ask the **Educational Psychologist** to comment on the impact of chronic stress on an adolescent.

Educational Psychologists might as well not be there if they aren't going to intervene on behalf of a child's mental well-being.

If anybody has an awareness of how the future might pan out for an autistic adolescent, it must surely be this group of people.

They should never be just an erudite rubber stampers of quasi-inclusion.

In my experience they are the group of professionals who currently display the biggest gap between their potential and their actual use. Matters of cost should **not** be part of their deliberations.

It is appalling that the gains made in the relative haven of the primary school might, for lack of perspective, care and planning, be lost in the jungle of a mainstream secondary school.

It's a bit like spending years restoring a unique vintage car and then one day entering it in a demolition derby!

One more thing: Just because we parents have 'rights' e.g. a mainstream placement, we don't always *have* to exercise those rights.

Especially if our 'rights' impinge on somebody else's even more basic rights. Children have the *right* not to be driven to despair, depression and suicide.

Is it possibly a wee bit paradoxical that most of us end up fighting for - and being delighted with - the cheapest educational option available.

We're not being manipulated are we?

The lobby for 'Inclusion' remains strong

In one school I taught in there was a student, James M, who had Cerebral Palsy. In his case it affected his movement not his speech. James was a real character and an integral part of my PSHE programme for years. He would give a talk about what it was like to have a disability and field questions from other children. He was brilliant. And it only cost me a KFC every time he did his talk. But a child with autistic traits is a completely different challenge for a mainstream school and vice-versa.

Three groups of adults collude to create this trend towards 'inclusion': Parents, politicians, and bureaucrats.   Parents, because a mainstream placement represents an affirmation of their child's progress and potential. And also because it is their 'right'. When asked 'What is your understanding of the term inclusion?'

Five times as many parents of young autistic adults cited - *'to take part in community life* - as opposed to - *'going to a mainstream school'.* Perhaps it is just too difficult to appreciate this when they are younger, and we are still hoping that something resembling a silver bullet will be found in 'big' school.

Politicians support *Inclusion,* because it *seems* equitable or because its cheapness delivers elbow room for populist tax cuts.

Bureaucrats support Inclusion because it eases pressure on their budgets. Each child taught in the mainstream saves money.

In a TES article (10/10/04), Martin Whittaker talks of Headteachers coming under increasing pressure to make their schools more *inclusive.*

The government's strategy **'Removing Barriers to Achievement'** says that effective inclusion...requires a positive attitude towards children who have difficulties in school.

Manchester, for example, is actively promoting inclusion with a new kite-mark!

A new postgraduate course is now helping heads, deputies, and middle management to achieve the inclusion agenda; notice there is no mention of the *poor bloody infantry* in the classroom: **'Managing Inclusion and Special Education'** is the first course of its kind in the country. It has been described as *'groundbreaking'* by Ofsted. (I think they mean this to sound inviting!)

Even within a disability grouping there will be huge differences between individuals. As the one-time British shadow education secretary Tim Collins said

" Every child is unique. Many will benefit from mainstream education but sadly many will not. .. there's no doubt that the Government came in with a very strong ideological commitment in pretty much all circumstances. That has been a major factor in the continuing programme of closure of special schools."

Because this lobby seems oblivious to the very different needs of very different children it is difficult to conclude it is not essentially finance-driven.

We have to take a step back to see the big picture.

" There is a fundamental question: to what end is inclusion being promoted in education? Our evidence shows that post-19 there is very little for most adults to look forward to ". (Inclusion and Autism: Is it working? by Barnard Prior and Potter NAS 2000).

There really is some really fuzzy thinking underlying the '*Inclusion'* lobby – is it school or society that we are trying to 'include' them in?

Isn't it a damn sight easier to 'include' a socially proficient sane person in society!

As parents we should *play the long game* and not get dragged into chasing short term and transient objectives. Some policy makers seem to think *placement* in a mainstream secondary school and *social inclusion* are the same thing. Whilst for some autistic children these two things will actually be mutually exclusive. In reality most parents would happily settle for their child's tolerably successful integration into the community. To pretend that a placement in a mainstream secondary school is a necessary prerequisite to **inclusion** in society is arrant nonsense; it may even cause the opposite to happen.

A national curriculum could never deliver for every individual.

The second most difficult job I ever had in teaching involved setting up a makeshift 'inclusion unit' for a group of Y9s half way through the academic year. The children concerned were causing havoc in many lessons and were at risk of exclusion. This was one of Blair's 'saints and heroes' moments. **'Challenging'** is a word schools try to avoid in job adverts because they know we know what it means. This was 'challenging' and the reasons why it was 'challenging' were far from challenging to pin down: An overwhelming consensus of teachers view Y9 (13/14 yr olds) as the most difficult year to teach. These Y9 children were the most difficult of the most difficult in Y9. And this very good school took in children from the poorest borough of the 8,814 boroughs in England.

But the single biggest factor making life 'challenging' for all of us was the curriculum I had to deliver : Year 9 is a SATs year .

At a time when we should be employing all our teaching skills to avoid disaffection we are drilling them to sit tests that many of them will 'fail' (relative to their peers).

The best afternoon I had with them (2-hour slot) was when they - electronic tags on legs - brought their crochet work in from their art lesson .I let them carry on - we just had a chat.

The activity was simple and repetitive and soporific - sufficiently so to offset the various chemicals imbibed the night before.

(God knows what they'd had.)

It was a strange experience - a bit like that game of yuletide football on the Somme in 1914. Hostilities re-commenced the day after too!

After 18 years in the national curriculum straightjacket, Politicians in England are making noises about trusting teachers again with the curriculum.

If it ever happens, this is a good thing.

Increased flexibility in the system is long overdue.

Current provision for many autistic children is a waste of valuable time.

It's not as if you *need* 10 GCSE subjects to get into University.

And the stresses and strains of achieving this can be great and ultimately counter-productive. Just to go through a few subjects and the possible pitfalls:

Drama: based on abstract concepts and group work; involves movement of body in space. Can be very noisy.

PE: difficulty screening out background noise in the gym; poor ball skills; difficulty changing; coping with 'Locker room' mentality; macho teachers (dwindling minority… many are brilliant with less able children nowadays); ungainly movements leading to derision; visual-spatial deficits.

Team games: Getting dirty can upset some autistic children; not understanding the rules; being picked last.

Maths –academic content / dyscalculia / staff shortages and discipline in supply teachers lessons **Food tech**.: using initiative; dangerous utensils.

RE – abstract concepts.

Art - dyspraxia? Problems with sequencing.

Technology; instructions /noises / dexterity/ dangerous tools.

English – comprehension, use of symbolism, abstract concepts

Science – 1 in 3 secondary schools do not conduct practical science lessons because of poor behaviour in the labs; they can't trust the children not to throw chemicals at each other. Guess who the target would be if they did.

Information Technology – brilliant apart from the spreadsheet sums if you have dyscalculia.

That said, every child with AS will have his or her favourite subject. Sometimes the success in this discipline can be prodigious relative to peers.

My son's fascination with **History** must, in part at least, been due to people telling him he was good at it. This would, in turn, have been down to his proficient long-term memory. History was the best thing in the curriculum from his perspective. So the ever so keen young history teacher who assured me at a parents evening that my son would 'never make an academic historian', was missing the point somewhat. (And was therefore blissfully unaware of my inclination to throttle him.)

Much of the rest of his school experience was - no reflection on the excellent personnel - was irrelevant, stressful, or both.

The pace of delivery, the movement, the amount of things to be carried, the language used to start lessons, the classroom conflicts, the idiosyncratic expectations of teachers, all compound the difficulty of dealing with this largely irrelevant material.

There *has* to be a very good reason for educating them in this environment. A curriculum designed for a nation rather than for an individual *isn't* a very good reason.

A curriculum ought to reflect its ultimate objectives.

For most parents and children the objectives of education are straightforward enough: a good set of exam results. It is *so* easy to get swept along with this conventional and widespread position
But, as the **Irish Task force on Autism** points out:

The curriculum content should be based on long-term goals, so that the usefulness of each item is evaluated in terms of its long-term benefits.

So parenting an autistic child requires a reality check on the school curriculum on offer. Don't expect the initiative to come from the school; left to its own devices an institution will plough on like an oil tanker and deliver what it is designed to deliver.

As we all know from experience much of what we learnt in school was purely 'academic'; a means to an end. That end being exam success. So it's hardly news that many people find, pub quizzes aside, a lot of the content of the curriculum to have been of little use in later life. In terms of its intrinsic value it might be considered a *waste of time*.

Autistic children do not learn much about anything in an incidental fashion. So there is little time to waste on 'academic' ballast – especially if projected exam grades will be opening no doors.

Even academically gifted students need do no more than 5 GCSE subjects – including Maths and English to fulfil the criteria for university entrance.

To call the present set-up ostrich-like does a disservice to ostriches.

Far too much time and energy being dissipated on stuff that confers minimal marginal benefit. Autistic children desperately need that time to be spent learning the fundamentals of. …life.

We need to audit the curriculum and ask

' What's the worse case scenario if he doesn't know this'.

The result of this audit would pare the national curriculum to the bone - making more elbow room for teaching the things that *really* matter to an autistic child. That an alternative curriculum needs to be established for autistic children is given further weight by the **Task Force on Autism**. They argue:

"For all pupils with ASDs, second level provision should take a 'whole person' view and have the flexibility to facilitate more than just 'classroom studies'. The following topics should be taught in all post-primary educational settings: living skills; independent living skills; social skills; family and community life; the world of work; individual development; sexuality; cognitive skills; coping with isolation, loneliness and peer rejection; coping with the social pressures

of adolescence; coping with all the changes of teachers subjects and classrooms; coping with unstructured time i.e. break-time, lunch-time etc; maintaining a level of self-esteem ; maximisation of talents and practical skills ;coming to terms with the implications of AS/HFA....computer/IT skills ;arts/culture participation appreciation and enjoyment ; stress management ; roles and duties of employment ; organising of non-working periods." .

So if all of this needs to be addressed - something has to give.
And somebody with clout has to be pro-active in making it give.

Stress produces adverse short-term consequences.

In April 2005 the president of the newly forged Iraqi Parliament had to leave the ceremony to install a Prime Minister. He had forgotten the name of the man who was to be Prime Minister. If your mind has ever gone blank in an exam or interview you might empathise with this scenario. All of us are vulnerable to the stress hormone, cortisol; it is the body's natural response to stressful situations and has been shown to significantly impair memory retrieval. Possibly so we can ignore the small stuff and concentrate on 'fight or flight'.

A lot of recent research on stress gives cause for concern to parents of autistic children. Some of this research is focused on cortisol. Is this a contributory factor in my son's difficulty finding the right words sometimes? Is susceptibility to stress in general a key factor in autism? I don't know, but there is some evidence that it is.
Kathleen Taylor is a neuroscientist at Oxford University. Talking of human neurology in general she has come to the conclusion that,

"Stress affects the brain such that it makes people more likely to fall back on things they know well – stereotypes and simple ways of thinking. "

This bolt into familiar holes sounds very...familiar!

So our children **are** displaying a *normal* reaction to stress.
What *is* different is their extreme susceptibility to feel stress in situations where other children do not. The logic would be, therefore, to isolate the sources of the stress and eliminate them - unless we *really* enjoy monotonic monologues about Star Wars etc.

School corridors can be hugely stressful places for autistic children. A child who has become stressed en route to a lesson is at an immediate disadvantage in that lesson. The gap between the teacher's expectations in that lesson, and the child's ability to focus can lead to further tension and stress. The child may be 'closing down' and looking to therap themselves by talking about their speciality, whilst it is likely that Star Wars will not be the teacher's chosen topic for the lesson! So, seemingly out of the blue, a snowball of disaffection begins to grow. A distracted and uncooperative child will soon be subject to intervention by the teacher. Cajoling eventually giving way to disciplinary warnings. Many autistic children fear and resent 'unwarranted' threats of detention and the like. They are still in turmoil over the corridor incidents, trying to work out what happened and why.
Now some teacher is having a pop at them for something else.... generating more and more frustration with themselves and anybody else in the vicinity. All it takes is a jibe from a classmate and the blue touch paper is well and truly lit. This is not *wilfully* bad behaviour. It is the response of somebody who is stressed out beyond the point of coping because they are neurologically different. It is a response to a particular environment. An environment we put them in.

Autistic children in mainstream schools experience high levels of stress throughout the school day. Stress generates cortisol. Cortisol impairs learning. So is this *really* the best learning environment we can come up with for autistic children? Would an environment that didn't leave a student awash with cortisol be a better option?

Stress produces adverse long-term consequences.

A brief dose of stress, may, according to some psychologists, actually do us some good. It is thought that the process of periodically calling up our 'fight or flight' response tunes up our immune system. In contrast to this, exposure to chronic stress with no 'light at the end of the tunnel' has the opposite effect on our ability to ward off illness.

Evidence is growing that unrelenting stress can produce cortisol at a level that is toxic to the brain. Brain cells by the billion can be killed or injured. Over time excessive cortisol undermines the biochemical integrity of the brain. The rest of the body is adversely affected too: Professor Edward Suarez on behalf of Harvard Medical School cites the release of stress hormones as a key factor in heart attacks "Fifty per cent of those who have heart attacks do **not** have high cholesterol ".

The research also found that childhood trauma can cause heart problems later on.

(Apparently friendship, optimism, and laughter protect the heart and have healing effects. If their AS means friendship is difficult - we should be building in huge compensatory dollops of the other two)

The implications of the above render any 'cost-benefit' analysis redundant.
Situations that produce chronic stress must be avoided.
If the environment that generates that stress *cannot* be modified the only solution is not to dwell in that environment. Fulltime attendance at a mainstream secondary schools forces many autistic children to experience chronic levels of stress.

The internet is full of nightmarish anecdotes written by 'aspies' relating the hell that developed in their secondary school years.

As for the *'light at the end of the tunnel'* that might make it bearable? Remember how slowly the years go by when you are that age.

If you are approaching 'meltdown' at the age of 12 the prospect of being able to escape at the grand old age of 16 is of no use to you. If you are being teased and bullied remorselessly at the age of 13 it is of scant comfort to be told your peers will be less cannibalistic when they are 17.

So let's take stock. For many autistic children being at a mainstream secondary school involves operating with high levels of stress every day. We know chronic stress eventually impacts on the immune system and impairs mental and/or physical health.

So given this most appalling scenario how do we respond?

We put in place expensive support structures to keep them in..... The **same** environment.

Might this be a good point to step back and have a little re-think.

Even worse if the support itself is inherently stressful. In some cases this may be the case. Think back to when you were a teenager. Most adolescents are terrified of being singled out and are further stigmatised by being seen to need support. How would you have felt in school with a middle-aged helper sitting next to you. Teenagers with AS are often desperately trying to 'fit in' and being in the spotlight like this can be a total nightmare. Especially if the support teacher/assistant has little grasp on how the classroom 'feels' to an autistic child.

If you asked a committee to design a 'hell on earth' environment for somebody with Asperger Syndrome they would report back with... a mainstream secondary school.

Schools are bombarded by initiatives they cannot possibly comply with. Last week's focus may have been about bullying. This week's issue is keeping track of excluded bullies. Heads can lose their jobs if they fail to learn how to play the game. The first casualty of micro-management may be a Headteacher's job/health. Joint-first in the casualty stakes is integrity. Perception becomes everything. Spin is the order of the day. Get the flowers in Reception. Get the mission statement on the new sign at the gate. Specialise – unless you are a special school of course (in which case close down).

It's a charade teachers have been forced to take part in but they have learnt to play the game well. If you can double your A level 'A' grades by changing (competing) exam boards you do it. I did. And I got performance related pay for changing the address we sent the exam scripts to.

On radio 4 the other day a primary school teacher, his voice disguised, blew the whistle on how colleagues give children help during SATs in year 6. Secondary schools test again because they can't trust the results from the primary schools.

I know of a secondary Head who sent the difficult (AS?) children off on a school trip during an Ofsted inspection; this is common enough.

But this prestigious lady covered the tracks of her stilettos with fictitious minutes of a meeting that never took place – well before the Ofsted letter arrived! Staff were bribed and bullied into having their names on the fictitious meeting's minutes. It was made known that their references would be withheld for non-compliance. The woman concerned is still much lauded and sought out by the media as an educational expert!

I only mention this to highlight the fierce unrelenting grip that Ofsted and exam league tables has on what actually goes on in schools. The most important group of children in UK mainstream secondary schools are those who hover tantalisingly just below grade C at GCSE.

If a child with autism is operating within this target group it will get a disproportionate amount of support.

With the advent of de-industrialisation, children have morphed from factory fodder to league table fodder.

Not that there *wouldn't* be rejoicing in the special needs room for an autistic child that performed well.

But the criteria for success are narrow and must be set against the less measurable consequences of all this pressure.

Meanwhile, back in the Staffroom, we punch the air when we hear that a challenging child has been excluded for a few days. Been there. Done it. You would too – especially if you were due to teach him/her that morning.

It is into this narrowly focused environment that we send our children to be *included.*

Teachers are between a rock and a hard place. Whilst the vast majority will have an innate inclination to help a child with a disability, the climate they work in increasingly militates against it.

'Subject Fundamentalists'

….. are the worst type of teacher for a child with AS to encounter.

I know because I used to be one.

I believed passionately in the subject I taught and viewed children as empty vessels to be filled with this 'knowledge'.

I was like The Borg in Star Trek (I know lots about Star Trek): Resistance was futile.

I taught my subject **not** children.

I didn't give much thought to them as emergent personalities with complicated lives beyond the school gate.

As for different neurology…. forget it.

Yet without teachers possessing this narrow mindset, schools would not survive in their current form. Subject fundamentalists are the backbone of the system – conscientious and driven. Subject fundamentalists are very good teachers for the majority of students but *not* for autistic children . They can be very demanding in terms of quantity of work, homework, and rules. And be the source of sleepless nights for children who can't deliver.

Schools have pastoral systems too. If your child is lucky in their first year, they might get a young form tutor with energy, empathy, and enthusiasm to spare. If they are unlucky they might get me… press-ganged into dealing with the new intake whilst running a department.
Teachers are not perfect substitutes for each other.
Whether your child survives in the mainstream may depend on the form tutor they get. This shouldn't be left to chance.
It may be unless you make an issue of it.

Heads of year matter too…and they have their own spectrum of ability and interest. Some get to know the children very well and care a lot; others are just using the post as a springboard for further promotion.
As a parent you can't choose the year head but if you are being stonewalled ask to see the Deputy Head in charge of the pastoral system. It won't make you popular but it will put your child on the map for sensitive handling. And that's what matters.
Ideally the dialogue will have begun well before the transition to secondary school. In a 'good' school some of the issues will get through to some of the teachers but assume nothing. The lines of communication in a big school are complex and far from perfect. Write to each subject teacher individually to explain how best to handle your child. Make the tone collaborative not confrontational. Most will welcome the tips because it makes life easier.

When there is a problem – as there will be - give people the benefit of the doubt. Do you get it right all the time? And you haven't got a couple of dozen others to deal with.
Arranging a face-to-face early on will help but don't expect miracles; it'll still be a jungle for children with AS.

Homework can be the straw that breaks the camels back.

A recent suggestion that children be let off homework as long as they don't 'bunk off' school was greeted with howls of protest. In a UK television poll that followed up the suggestion, an amazing 99% said that we were too soft on children in general. This would indicate something of a rift between the generations cross-channel!

Whatever the general view, homework for a child with, AS can be the straw that breaks the camel's back. Coping with a high level of stress all day induces fatigue. It borders on cruel to expect several more hours of *academic* work to be completed in the evening when they are shattered.

The work to be done may also be imperfectly recorded due to their immature executive skills – adding to the stress of actually completing it. Anxiety about going in next day with work incomplete is very difficult to shift before bedtime. Sleep patterns, already a problem for many, can be further disturbed by such anxiety.

So teachers next day have to cope with a sleepy nervy teenager who presents a half-baked homework and even less ability to concentrate in class. All hell can break lose if a knackered 'aspie' meets a 'subject fundamentalist' whose washing machine flooded that morning. It's a lose-lose situation. Of all the interventions on behalf of an adolescent with AS, an individualised homework schedule is the easiest to implement; the potential benefits from such an approach can be huge. Many schools will operate this policy readily...even if Joe and Josephine Public disapprove of such flexibility.

Why did the 14 year old cross the road?

Answer: Because somebody told them not to.

In the myriad of potential stressors in school the single biggest stressor for an autistic teenager *is* ...a group of neuro-typical teenagers (perhaps 'neuro-transient' might be a better phrase for all teenagers since they should have *'danger: work in progress'* notes posted on their foreheads.)

Children between the age of 12 and 16 represent the biggest challenge an autistic person will *ever* face.

Interacting with this most volatile community is enormously stressful for somebody who doesn't understand the 'rules of engagement' - especially since those rules are as invariable as clouds. If you are 0.5% adrift of what is expected you **will** be excluded – and it won't be a polite invitation to 'go away'. This will be the daily lot of many autistic people in secondary school. You are surrounded by noisy smelly gangly arms and legs that might do you harm verbally or physically at a time of their choosing.

But to some extent they can't help annoying the rest of us.

Brains are very complicated things - not least during adolescence.
Apparently a second wave of grey matter is created at puberty.
This is followed by a neurological pruning which (I imagine) is akin to getting your computer de-bugged and upgraded.
The frontal lobes, which control 'executive functions' such as self-control, judgement, emotional regulation, organisation and planning, undergo the greatest changes between puberty and adulthood.
Moving from back to front, the **last** part of the brain to get unscrambled is the bit that governs the emotions and the inter-personal stuff.
Sensory functions also get a makeover at this time.

Sharon Begley 'Getting inside a teen brain' Newsweek 28/2/00
also highlights research from McLean Hospital, Boston. They have found that many teenagers are unable to empathise with other people's emotions. Their brains are failing to integrate visual clues with an appropriate response.
So they can see you are angry but are incapable of responding appropriately.

Does this also sound a bit familiar!!! .

Yes it does.

Professor David Skuse from University College London would agree.

His research with 1,600 children and teenagers indicated that the brain re-wiring that kicks in during puberty renders children 'temporarily autistic'.

These 'neuro –typicals' experiencing mid 'brain chemistry maelstrom' are the peers we are hoping will *teach* our autistic children social skills!!

Expecting an autistic child to learn social skills from their *re-wiring* peers is a bit like asking George Bush to teach environmental studies. We perhaps *misoverestimate* them.

So.... our kids don't get more like other peoples kids just because they spend time in the same building; in fact *their* kids get more like *our* kids!!!

And even if autistic children did take on board the social skills of a typical teenager, are these really the rules of engagement that we would want them to employ in adulthood!

From one perspective the autistic child is only 'failing' because of our insistence that they operate in this *peculiar* environment - the likes of which will not encountered again for the rest of their life!

(Do *you* work in a room with people who are all the same age as you?)

The '*but he'll miss out on social skills* ' argument against home education wobbles a bit at this point.

That he will certainly miss out on a few anti-social ones is very true!

"What on earth made me assume that the role models he would have would be good ones. The fact is, my child, who lacks any degree of cunning guile or

cruelty, has been exposed to all those unpleasant qualities..." The Inclusion Illusion - Vivien Sheffield (www.mugsy.org).

In any case the only times sanctioned for social interaction are those dreaded break times when chronic anxiety is a more likely outcome than enhanced social skills. To *truly* '**include**' a child it is necessary to 'fix' the environment to suit the child. This would unfortunately require most of the other 1500 children to stay at home! Social success is much more likely to be achieved in carefully engineered settings with vetted individuals.

Furthermore, people with Aspergers are not the only ones who are susceptible to mental health problems. As mentioned earlier, the mental health of teenagers in general has sharply declined in the last 25 years. The rate of emotional problems such as anxiety and depression has risen markedly for adolescents according to the biggest time trend study conducted in Britain (Institute of Psychiatry, Kings College London and the University of Manchester)

"We are doing something particularly unhelpful for adolescent mental health in Britain"

– Sharon Witherspoon, deputy director of the Nuffield foundation that funded the research.

The charity Childline have highlighted the increasing trend of children to self-harm. Teachers who have been in the profession since the seventies generally agree that schools are an increasingly challenging environment to work in. According to the Home Office crime and justice survey 2003, 1 in 4 boys aged 14-17 can be classified as prolific or serious offenders. The fall-out from these problems does not get left at the school gate. According to the latest musings from Ofsted, the proportion of schools maintaining generally 'good behaviour' has fallen from three-quarters to two-thirds in recent times. 1000 schools are failing to improve fast enough – whatever that means.

Over 300 schools are in 'special measures' with stress levels through the roof as embattled management seek to hang on to their jobs.

Even in leafy suburbs many a lesson looks and sounds nothing like the ones you get on the teachers TV channel!

The causation of these problems is beyond the remit of this book but the implications for autistic children should be noted.

Many disaffected young people – surprise, surprise - 'grow out' of their difficulties when they leave school (and will happily buy you a pint in the pub if they see you) …

But in the meantime

   (a) discipline in many schools has become more difficult to maintain
   (b) the peer group is even more volatile than it used to be.
   (c) Neither of these factors makes life easier for an autistic child already struggling to cope socially.

As a teacher the last thing I want in my already challenging classroom is a child with autistic traits - especially if an inspector is sitting at the back of the room with a clipboard.

And it isn't just teachers that don't want autistic children in the classroom.

Studies show that a big minority of secondary aged pupils were concerned about ridicule by peers if they maintained contact with pupils with disabilities. As with teachers, peer reticence applies much more to people who have intellectual and emotional deficits, rather than physical disabilities.

There is I think a strong (and growing?) case for keeping our children out of harm's way, at least until other people's children grow up a bit.

Why Bullying is like radioactivity.

Bullying is like radioactivity because: It's often *invisible* (to adults); the effects of exposure are cumulative; there is a critical amount that can be fatal; the only *real* solution is to stay out of the danger zone.

I met a young man called Paul in Westport, Co. Mayo. last week He wasn't autistic but he hadn't gone to school from the age of 12. He'd had a few drinks. I'd only just met him – we were complete strangers. Yet the first thing he wanted me to know was that the bullies hadn't won. He could strip down a tractor and put it back together – and was making a few bob breeding dogs too. He was getting married soon as well. If only the bastards could see him now. Paul would have been in his mid-twenties. Nice lad.

The recent initiative in England - asking children to wear yellow bands to show they were *anti-bullying* was well intentioned but not the best idea ever. …hello I'm *not* actually a wildebeest myself, but I know somebody who is.

But it's not really what's on their wrists that matters; it's what's in their heads and hearts.
And given their heads can be a bit frazzled during adolescence we're forced to fall back on just how alert, imaginative and responsive the adults in the building are.
Vulnerable children depend on the adults having the time energy and inclination to make the environment difficult and dangerous for bullies.
By stretching teachers to the limit Politicians have diminished the time energy and inclination to go the extra mile.
When Kenneth Baker took away a week of my holidays in the 1980's, I put away my football whistle on Saturday mornings. …And had a lie-in.
You just cannot abuse people's goodwill without getting a response.
If I am unlikely to get a free period in the day I *cannot* give up my lunchtime to structure it for an autistic child or make the toilets safe for toileting.

Meanwhile the Headteacher will probably be too busy concocting bullshit (bid writing) to get the money to keep the place going, to get involved in nitty-gritty stuff like bullying.

So when Heads say (as they often do after a *tragedy)* that they are not aware of a bullying problem in the school …it's true.

Dr Emily Lovegrove, a research fellow from the University of the West of England who teaches anti-bullying strategies in schools and businesses, has spent the past five years interviewing more than 1,000 adolescent victims. She said:

'There are bullies in every class, looking for targets, but I have found that the way they pick one child over another generally comes down to one simple issue: that of the victim's appearance, body language and dress. '

Dr Lovegrove also found that almost one in four of her interviewees admitted to feeling uncomfortable around those who looked different.

The solution is to change your demeanour, body language, and appearance. Making eye contact with the bully is also a good idea.

If this analysis is correct then autistic children are on a hiding to nothing – literally.

Their built in propensity to avoid eye contact, their ungainly movements, their lack of motivation to follow fashions, their difficulties with banter – in fact just about every aspect of their being cries **'Wildebeest.'**

And a quarter of your peers are going to let you know about *your* shortcomings because you arouse **their** insecurity about their own appearance.

Would you like to be sent into this bear-pit on a daily basis?

There is, apparently, a phenomenon whereby a bullied person can be a 'Provocative Victim'. This entails bringing the problem upon yourself by your behaviour. As the behaviour of our children is *not* wilful, but the result of neurological factors, I think we can say this tag is inappropriate.

That said, though, we have to acknowledge that some of the behavioural traits can be very annoying and it is unsurprising that less tolerant teenagers are irked and respond in kind.

Sometimes an autistic child that feels threatened by jostling pupils in a corridor will get their retaliation in first.

Many teenagers with autism are quick to involve teachers – as they are told to. This doesn't endear them to other children. And, like the boy that cried wolf too often, diminishing returns will set in with the adults. They will need a long-suffering form tutor to keep on giving solace and counselling.
The situation is likely to deteriorate fast when a less empathetic member of staff is involved.

Professor Mona O'Moore from TCD anti-bullying centre has highlighted the impact of abusive behaviour on children citing it as a cause of low self-worth, under-achievement, and early school leaving.
These in turn can lead to depression self-harm and suicide

"…some kids have said the most effective way to combat bullying is to commit suicide"

In Ireland in 2003 120 people between the ages of 15 and 24 committed suicide.

Dr Maria Lawlor (NEHB) and John Harpur (NUI Maynooth) point out that,

"Persistent bullying of children with Asperger Syndrome makes them prone to suicidal thoughts, depression, and school absenteeism…students [with AS]

are 10 times more likely to be bullied several times a week ...mainstream schools [are] ill-equipped to deal with their needs.

So bullying **will** be a problem for an autistic child in a mainstream school. It **will** happen and it **will** be almost impossible to eliminate. Suicides have happened as a result of it.

This factor alone, calls into question the wisdom of exposing autistic children to unsupervised contact with large numbers of intolerant teenagers.

When we get it wrong they suffer – for a long time.

I recently read a letter in The Independent (UK version). I believe it would lose its impact if it were paraphrased. It reads,

" Almost 40 years ago as a boy of 10, I was subjected to persistent bullying at a new school. The problem became so intolerable that I was packed off to the child psychiatrist to find out what was wrong with me and why I was causing the bullies to target me. Of course this had no effect on the bullies and the bullying. But there was one positive outcome for me: the psychiatrist's IQ tests revealed that I had the highest IQ he had ever measured. Here was something of my very own that could not be spoiled or taken away by the bullies, and it was a great impetus to me. Twenty years later I had earned a PhD. But I still have the deep and intractable depression that the bullying caused. I cannot use my intellectual and academic skills to earn myself an income, but I live at the state's expense on benefits, isolated at home with my books and strange interests, keeping myself quietly and irrelevantly away from a society I cannot cope with.
Dr S.K

The writer doesn't mention AS. But there are several indicators in the letter to suggest undiagnosed AS. It is a truly sad tale of a life unfulfilled. Forty years on, not much has changed.

We need to listen to what autistic people in their late teens and twenties say about their time at school.

Autistic adults often reflect that autism is not something they 'have'; it is an integral part of who they are. There are several supportive and campaigning 'Autistic Pride' websites out there. We have to listen carefully to their experiences so as to inform our interventions with younger autistic people: If we don't understand their view of the world we should not be wading in to change it. We should at least try to walk in *their* moccasins before we exercise the power we have when they are children. The lack of empathy in autism currently operates in both directions. One of the biggest dangers is that an autistic child will end up in a secondary school full of people like me. Or me that was that is!

I must have had a fair few students with Aspergers Syndrome in my classes over the years. I just didn't know it at the time. Neither did most of them, I think. Of the five children that *now* stand out in my mind as autistic, I believe I did no harm to two, was driven up the wall by another, helped one, and couldn't catch the other.

Anecdotal evidence of hurtful experiences is not in short supply on 'aspie' websites. In an effort to pull things together the excellent **AS-IF** website reports on a wider survey of 275 adults with AS. The responses to the following questions were as follows:

- I think if my education was better suited to me my life would be very different - 78% agreed

- I nearly always had a supportive group of friends throughout school – 89% disagreed

- I experienced traumatic things at school that I suspect may be psychologically damaging – 69% agreed

- My teachers were fair and usually made an effort to understand me – 76% disagreed

- I was frequently the target of teasing and bullying at school – 71% agreed

AS-IF Questionnaire for adults with AS (275 respondents)

One more point can be made here: Many children with AS are sticklers for rules and regulations and would dearly love to stick to school rules and avoid trouble. They just don't know how. Contrary to the perception of many, they are **not** born troublemakers. Exactly the opposite is the case.

As I was writing just now, I had radio 4 on in the background. Gardeners Question Time to be specific. I couldn't help but latch on to one impassioned plea for help. A woman was beside herself because all the branches on her monkey-puzzle tree were pointing in the *same* direction! My first thoughts were …best ask the monkey for the solution. But yes, a small amount of jealousy crept in vis-à-vis the relative magnitude of her '*problem*'.

However, on reflection, I finished up feeling admiration for somebody who has decided to focus on things in this world that *can* be fixed.

One in five children with autism are excluded from mainstream school at some point.

That shouldn't be happening.
Like the monkey-puzzle tree – it's something we could put right.

Professionals should be 'on tap not on top'.

In our dreams.
For two reasons.
Because they come and go with funding and promotions etc
and when you do get one they are the 'expert' and mum and dad are deferential for the most part.

Parents need to be empowered by the professionals they come into contact with. At the very least they should listen to what we have to say very carefully. We are the key workers in the equation because -

   (a) we care the most

   (b) we are on call 24/7

   (c) we don't start afresh with new children each September

   (d) we don't get promoted and move away

   (e) only we can sanction experiential risks.

Parental energy is a scarce resource. Getting and keeping support and therapy for autistic children currently uses up far too much of that energy. Providing effective interventions on behalf of children with AS is a science in its infancy. We could do with help but could do without being patronised or ignored. Having a child who is 'nearly normal' is - in the early days at least - a recipe for pats on the head and reassurance rather than action.
And this is dangerous given what can transpire during adolescence.

The situation in Ireland is worse than the UK in terms of nailing down a diagnosis through the public health system.

Most people are driven to 'go private' to get a diagnosis.

After that support and advice is just as spasmodic on both sides of the Irish Sea.

Given the lack of a template for the child with Aspergers Syndrome it is all the more important for deference to run from professionals to parent and not vice-versa.

Professionals who don't listen *carefully* to parents ... aren't.

Stereotypes are a bad thing.

But here goes anyway.

In a whistle-stop tour of my own limited experiences.

Speech therapists tend to be thoroughly professional. Calm, reassuring and focused. Willing to explain all the complicated bits in their reports. Keen to highlight and build on the 'positives'.

Occupational therapists have been good for us too; slightly scary people, but good at what they do and very very helpful. Strong minded and caring. Only too happy to enlist us into their dark arts.

Doctors can be inclined to patronise and bluster if unsure. I'm sure my doctor thinks I'm a hippy; why else would I be keeping my son at home to educate him!!

Teachers are under so much pressure it is unrealistic to expect too much but..

Teachers at parents evenings - please just tell us something nice and let us go home with something good to hang onto; something for us to tell *them* which builds up our child's self-esteem and confidence.

I really don't give a rat's bottom if he doesn't know how to do six-figure grid references. Let's take all the weaknesses as read: If he is still there with you and isn't showing signs of depression then you are doing something very right. Don't spoil it by thinking you need to revert to conventional comments; this is an unconventional situation. As a rule of thumb avoid using the word 'but'….

A parent once shut me up in mid-parent-evening- babble. " I've only got two questions. Is he happy? Is he doing his best?"

I wish they'd all have been as focused as that. I'd have got home a lot earlier.

And she was dead right just to concentrate on those two things.

We need to get back to basics.. back to treating children as more than just the sum of their levels. And we need to chuck the bloody levels and league tables out the window.

Educational psychologists could be an even bigger part of the solution. If a child were to have one ally in all the politics and systems and egos, you would like it to be the professional with the greatest insight into how chronic stress impacts on young people. (Did I slag them off earlier – I forget) Powerful in inverse proportion to the time they spend with our children, I would really want them to be

(a) the child's biggest protection from 'the system' whether it be pushy parents or grumpy classroom teachers.

(b) sensitive to the open wound that parents have re. their child's disability - not to be too glib or detached, as if they are inured to the human condition in all it's manifestations

(c) willing and able to explain to parents the options at their disposal - spelling out clearly the possible implications of the alternatives.

(d) totally *up front* about the possibility of depression in adolescence.

(e) Not acting as a proxy beancounter for the providers

Professionals that deal with parents need to be as sensitive as possible.

Just because we look as though we are coping doesn't mean that we are totally reconciled to our child's disability. Imagine there is an invisible knife in our guts that you should try to avoid twisting. Our resilience is born of necessity but you can give it a boost or you can peel some of it away.

We need you to validate our efforts and positively build on our existing solutions. We really can do without throwaway lines that knock the stuffing out of us.

Horses for courses

I was never going to be a champion pole-vaulter. The legs were too short; a genetic endowment that a pole-vaulting coach would spot immediately and thereby desist from fruitless endeavour on both our parts. If some less astute mentor had persisted in trying to make me into a champion pole-vaulter it would have been very annoying. After a number of frustrating sessions I would probably suggest we part company lest I be driven to find an alternative use for the pole.

Autistic children don't get to opt out. They go where we put them.

Why is it, given our children are differently endowed, that we insist on them learning in almost exactly the same manner as their neuro-typical peers. Are we pretending they are **not** different. Does it suit our sensitivities to pretend as much; will we wake up one morning and find it's all been a bad dream and as long as we don't step off the straight and narrow things will be ok. Or is it just a sheer absence of imagination and deference in the face of 'off the shelf' education provision that already exists 100 metres away as bricks, mortar, and a fancy mission statement. Are we afraid of sideways looks from regular folk if we don't deliver our children into the arms of the people who know best; the 'professionals'.

Ok. Thanks. Did me good that. Now where's that bloody candle ?

Looking for the bloody candle

I have a great memory. I remember very little.

But I do remember the car.

Sean wouldn't do anything jointly for longer than a few seconds: constantly running away; squirming to get off the knee; ignoring exhortations to put shapes in holes – except the cassette in the car's cassette player. I didn't have a clue why he was transfixed by the cassette player in the Ford Sierra – pushing the tape in then pushing the button to get it out. Over and over again

But I was grateful that something - anything - could retain his interest for a while. I was grateful for the respite I got while he was doing it. He would have happily spent the day pushing the tape in and getting it out. There were times when I let him.

He was about two and a half.

One of my few other vivid memories is of me holding him up to the apple tree and helping him to pluck an apple and then drop it in a box. I was chuffed to bits. The best job I ever had was picking strawberries in Norfolk – earning beer money for the evening.

He could pick strawberries in Norfolk too - like his Dad.

But what would he do in the winter?

If only his first primary school teacher had the insight the child's parents crave when they nervously drop him off on that first day.

If his first teacher had perfect insight s/he would say to us:

Let's get to know him; tell me what he enjoys – tell me what he's interested in – what he's good at. First we'll do him no harm; we'll accept that his behaviour is communication. We know he isn't wilful – he has difficulties because of his neurological endowment; we know he reacts badly to a noisy environment.

Super teach would go on in sage-like fashion:

You, not me, are the key worker. I'll have a new batch next September. If he needs a day off to settle his head down – fair enough. Just write me a note I'll jot down stuff for you too. It won't be easy but you need to cast a cold eye on conventional rites of passage; question the efficacy of institutions, experts, and interventions; put *your* ego in a box and lock it away so that decisions reflect **his** best interests not yours; play the long game; fear the future less; minimise his exposure to chronic stress; minimise his exposure to predators; engineer more artificial success to boost self-esteem; celebrate his progress irrespective of what his peers are up to; externalise his difficulties and collaborate with him on strategies to minimise them ; identify and nurture his strengths . You like football – well, play the way you are facing.

The teacher of the new millennium would tell us to view the process more as 'getting the excellence out of him than putting the excellence into him'.

Most importantly, this jaw-droppingly insightful person would say.
"He'll be fine with us once we get to know him …".
Wow.

People with autism have a neurology that is different to the norm: Areas of the brain that govern interaction with the 'outside world' function differently when you are autistic.

Many different kinds of people can be autistic. The conventional wisdom is to view autism as a *spectrum* disorder that can accommodate any underlying level of intellectual ability. At one end of the spectrum is the person who will never develop speech and has significant additional needs. This is sometimes referred to as 'Classic' (or Kanner's) autism. At the other end are people with second level qualifications, degrees and PhD's. This is the high functioning end of the spectrum in terms of academic functioning. People at this end are sometimes said to have 'Aspergers Syndrome'.

Using the current rates of incidence there are between 24 and 60 million people in the world operating at this end of the spectrum. And they are as different from each other as any two 'neuro- typical' people would be.

"Oh no…not another bloody syndrome."

I recently came across this whinge in a TES chatroom for teachers.
They were discussing declining standards of behaviour in schools.
There was a general consensus that it had all gone too far – the 'excuses' even more so than the behaviour!
I believe it was 'conduct disorder' that was the straw breaking the camels back. Various cynical comments were made about 'new' syndromes and what should be done to the little shits instead. I wasn't shocked. I'd been listening to, and making, similar comments for a quarter of a century myself.
To be fair Aspergers Syndrome (AS) didn't get mentioned explicitly, but I half expected one of them to say that 'it wasn't around when we were at school'. To be even fairer they would have been right.

In 1944 Hans Asperger, an Austrian paediatrician, was trying to fathom a group of boys. They had the characteristics described above and …

"They make their parents miserable and their teachers despair".

Hans Asperger and a 'little professor' (Wikipedia)

Asperger wrote a paper and described the condition as 'Autistic Psychopathy'. About the same time another Austrian, Leo Kanner, was independently working with a wider spectrum of children .He used the term 'Autistic' to describe their difficulties. Kanner's work was immediately available in English (Classic Autism is sometimes called Kanner Autism.)

Pre-Rainman this kind of autism held sway in the public perception of autism. Asperger's work, written in German, was not translated into English for nearly 40 years.

Lorna Wing, an English psychiatrist with an autistic daughter, wrote a paper in 1981 highlighting Aspergers work, refining it, and changing the label by way of tribute to the man's work. Thus Asperger Syndrome was born.

It has been 'around' for less than thirty years.

Neuro-diversity, however, has been around a bit longer or - as they say in Lancashire - since Adam were a lad.

(Adam did not have Asperger Syndrome. If he did he would have stuck rigidly to the rules and not taken a bite out of the apple... and as a stickler for honesty he would have 'shopped' Eve as the instigator of the apple biting.)

There is a school of thought that people with autistic neurology were present at all history's major turning points.

Michelangelo and Einstein were, according to Professor Michael Fitzgerald of Trinity College Dublin, probably autistic.

'Michaelangelo may have been Renaissance Rain Man'

the newspaper article headlined. God knows how Michelangelo and Einstein would have fared in an English secondary school circa 2006. No doubt both would have scored badly in their Year 9 geography SATs.

If they were operating just below the level likely to net them 5 grade C GCSE's they would have been invited in for Saturday lessons on 6-figure grid references. And been mentored by a senior member of staff to motivate them to become useful jack of all trades - thus securing the position in the league table, the head's job and the teacher's performance related pay. Mike might be counselled to drop Art to finish his history coursework and Bert could take maths early to get it out of the way.

Maybe, given the increasing numbers of people with this 'new' syndrome, a process of natural selection is at work in favour of people with 'high functioning autism'.

Would it be such a bad thing to have such honest people in charge of the planet: -

"Hello George.

"Hello Tony.. there are no WMD and it's all about oil."

"I know that George. Shall we sign up to Kyoto and cut the demand for oil."

"Yes, Tony that would be most efficacious."

So, colleagues, we did have people at school with Aspergers Syndrome. They got slaughtered back then, just like they do now. We should know. We did the slaughtering. The neurology isn't new; only the nomenclature makes it seem so.

It's an empathy deficit.

It seems to be an asymmetrical criticism of autistic people that *they* do not understand *us*. But the lack of empathy goes in both directions. The difference is that *we* have the neurology to be empathetic. Autistic people don't start out with that endowment. Their neurology imposes a 'Theory of Mind' deficit or delay (many believe it is not a life-long deficit.) I found this concept confusing when I first came across it. . It's sometimes phrased as '*lack of imagination*'.

But it **doesn't** mean he can't envisage battling alongside Jean Luc Piccard on the bridge of the starship Enterprise. It **does** mean he would have more in common with the star trek character Data than that nice lady who reads minds. She is an 'empath' which is exactly what he isn't.
(An adolescent Trekkie looking over my shoulder has just told me her name is Diana Troy). Well, Diana Troy knows that other people have thoughts and feelings, and that life can be made easier by finding out what those thoughts and feelings are.

There is a story that highlights this; a riverboat gambler was in a head to head high stakes poker game. He had tried to bluff his opponent out of the game but this had failed. A strong breeze came along and wafted one of his cards into the river. He waited a split-second then jumped in after it. Having nearly drowned in order to retrieve it, he sat back down at the table.
His opponent folded his hand immediately!
If there is no need for me to spell out the two gamblers thoughts and actions you are *probably* not autistic.

Most of the messages we transmit are far subtler than this. But subtle or not, they would be of little interest to a person with autistic neurology.

A more conventional illustration of this theory of mind deficit/delay is readily available on the internet. Put the *Sally and Anne test* in a search engine.

70

Lack of a 'Theory of Mind' explains why all young children can come out with comments that are embarrassing. Around about the age of four neuro-typical children start to understand that other people have thoughts and feelings and that taking them into account might be a good idea if you want a nice prezzy at Christmas. This doesn't happen when children are autistic. My son was the nicest person: I had to teach him how to be duplicitous, how to assess the impact of what he said on other people; how to judge different social situations and where appropriate tell half-truths and white lies.

Since we're big and they are small, the main emphasis seems to be in 'fixing' them to empathise with us. But our lack of empathy towards them is as much of a problem and gets a lot less attention. And we *can* help it. .

Scientists at the University of California have concluded that that the root of autism lies in the lack of neurons in the amygdala – the region of the brain that deals with social skills.

They found that men with autism have less neurons in that part of the brain. But it could be that the abnormalities are a *consequence* of a lack of social experience – and not the other way around. Even if the causality were lack of neurons causing incapacity the game isn't up. People recover from strokes. 5% of people source their language from the 'wrong' part of the brain. It would be more surprising if a young brain couldn't *find* a few ways around the initial difficulties; making new perhaps novel neural connections. Neuro-scientists have identified 're-wiring' taking place – albeit at snails pace – in the traumatised brains of car crash victims. Whether the new connections are the 'right' ones seem to be a bit hit and miss – some accident victims show no signs of recovery - but the law of averages suggest some degree of natural 'healing' should take place as the years go.

Why should our lads' traumas be totally impervious to the passage of time? There are still more questions than answers in this field.. but who cares? Let's take the **assumption** that some compensatory re-wiring *is* happening and run with it. It certainly ties in with my own experience. If it is, we should perhaps just give time the time it needs to do its work. And in the meantime – do as little harm as possible.

But as concerned parents and busy teachers we tend not to do this.
We push the river. ...and not always in the right direction

It isn't easy to chase a diagnosis that you desperately don't want.

I didn't know he was autistic six years ago when he was 11.

The question had been posed to two different Consultants before he was seven years old. Both had said that they didn't think he was autistic. I will not name the London institution concerned. Suffice to say they did not slay the dragon on either occasion.

I can understand the difficulty of a precise diagnosis when he was a few months shy of his fourth birthday.

True he had a language delay and it was noted that **'his articulation is very unclear and has a very limited range of sounds',** and he had experienced a **traumatic birth,** had **'a short attention span'** and **'when he is working on tasks that interest him.. he is not easy to direct into new channels'..'his emotions are not always appropriate.'And he displayed 'a degree of gaze avoidance'.** On the basis of these observations The consultant in 1991 could see why 'autism' had been suggested. But as he didn't show **social disinterest typical of the classical autistic child'** he felt '...**autism is not the appropriate label** 'and we could relax.

It would be *'.... worrying for a time'* but there was a **'good prognosis' ...all children experience big changes between 3 and 5.**

He wasn't autistic...it was official. It was very much a case of take the diagnosis and run. Better than winning the National Lottery.

In 1995 we were back. His Primary school had never met anybody quite like him. From his angle the feeling would have been mutual: Fathoming out what we all wanted him to do must have been a nightmare for him.

I appreciate that now. I didn't back then.

Back then – as a teacher myself- I was embarrassed to have presented the school with a disruptive child.

On top of that I was feeling deeply guilty for being embarrassed by him.

They were at a loss as to how best to help him.

And being the good people they were, they really *did* want to help.

At the time he would wander alone around the perimeter fence at break-time whilst games of football carried on next to him.

He was a good reader – same bedtime story every night - but his numeracy skills were almost non-existent.

His writing and drawing indecipherable.

At lunch he was a messy eater and couldn't dress himself too well after PE. In class he was for ever seeking attention and re-assurance.

Now and again he would come up with incredible *facts* or regale people with monologues.

Often these monologues would be delivered in overly ornate language. *Sometimes* these facts actually coincided with the lesson being taught!!

He was, in short, a total enigma. Unsurprisingly a hint of exasperation was to be found in his end of year reports. It was hardly surprising that a second opinion was sought at their behest. They really wanted to help him. They just didn't know how. Neither did I.

This second assessment involved talking to a different Consultant in the same institution but getting the same outcome. He had had significant speech therapy in the mean-time...progress was noted but **echolalia** was identified as a strategy he used: He was repeating the instructions for a task as he carried it out. He still does in a more subtle fashion. The report also cited...**gross coordination problems...poor balance...mixed laterality...short attention span** for things he finds difficult although he can concentrate quite well on things of his own choosing…gaze avoidance …

.. but again he was **not** autistic and mainstream education was the right environment for him - with a recommendation of occupational therapy.
This was 1995*!*
Whilst I can understand the caution of the first Consultant I find it hard to fathom why the second failed to mention the *possibility* of Asperger Syndrome.

This second assessment left me more bemused than elated.

It isn't easy to feel re-assured when you also feel confused and isolated. Did my son have some unique set of symptoms that nobody else on the planet had; that there was no name for. Consultants need to recognise the pain of this limbo that they sometimes leave parents in. Perhaps there should be a pre-diagnostic contract that absolves them from legal redress if they *overestimate* the problem. It might stop them from sitting on the fence.

Parents need to be told more than 'what it probably isn't'. How can they fight for support for their children with nebulous and over-cautious medical input? If the diagnosis is subsequently seen to be an overestimate (most unlikely) we can all rejoice in the extra resources it brought to bear on behalf of the child. There needs to be overt collaboration on this so that we err on the side of lack of caution.

Of course it's a gut wrenching shock to hear the word **autism** used by a third party in the same sentence as your child's name. But it isn't as if we turn up without this possibility in mind.

The sooner we know about *'it'* the sooner we can get on with minimising the impact *'it'* will be allowed to have on our child's life.

I had to head back to the (pre-internet) library; back to thumbing through books about ADD and Semantic-Pragmatic Disorder et al. I came across something called Dyspraxia. ...and there was a reasonable match between the typical presentation of Dyspraxia and my son's traits.

So I went back to the doctor and the teachers and told them what he had. Nobody seemed to argue much ...so son became *'Dyspraxic'.*

Actually this *is* the case.

It just isn't the full monty of the neurological story; that didn't arrive for another five and half years.

At the time, this under-diagnosis of Dyspraxia at least allowed for people in the school to up-skill in this related neurological disorder.

His gem of a support assistant delivered sessions of occupational therapy every day. And it took the pressure off him a bit e.g. when it came to getting changed for gym.

I resigned from one support group (for speech-impaired children) and joined another.

There is some discomfort with 'labelling' children but this rarely comes from people at the sharp end of things. As Charlotte Moore pointed out in the Guardian 6/2/02,

" Labels help. A label gets you a statement of special educational need, disability living allowance, sympathy and tolerance for misbehaviour. You get to occupy the moral high ground; a comfortable if sometimes lonely spot".

Most importantly the label acts as a compass; as such it reduces the number of blind alleys you go down.

If the Jesuits are right, the greatest '*good*'can be done before the age of seven. But anecdotal evidence suggests that for autistic children, the greatest damage can be done between the ages of 11 and 18.

This is the time when some families stop dealing with *just* a disability and start dealing with an **illness** *and* a disability. But it isn't as if the 'blues just come out of the blue': We **know** there are additional stressors in second level education for autistic children. We **know** adolescence brings a heightened sense of self. Put the two together and you have a double whammy that is just too much for some children to handle. We can't stop the onset of adolescence. But we *can* think twice about the environment we force them to operate in.

In the computer drafted diagnosis which – third time lucky – finally established his place on the autistic spectrum the Consultant warned, **"I think you are doing very well with x … young people like x …are in particular risk of mental health problems, anxiety, depression.**

This warning arrived nine years later than it could have done.
The Educational Psychologist, soon after, flagged up warning signs and asked for extra support from the LEA to prevent this happening.
He was in tears at the end of some days because he was
" much more aware of the problems he has and.. very self-conscious and displaying higher levels of anxiety."

Even before it became clear that the bureaucrats were going to drag their feet on the extra support, I resolved not to hang around.
He was going into Year 9 - a SATs year and stress levels would escalate accordingly.
I gave notice that he would leave his otherwise excellent secondary school at the end of the year.
I began to allow him more and more 'mental health' days off. Nobody argued with my decision to withdraw him, or chased us up over the *mental health* days.
Everybody in the school who knew and cared for him knew it was for the best.

Try this short-term memory exercise:

Look at this number: 754139
Now look away and say the number
Now say it backwards.

Now this number: 3853921
…but tell me your birthday first.

Most people's short-term memory skills are impaired by a distraction.

What must it be like to have distractions from all 5 senses coming at you whilst somebody is giving you complex instructions – possibly another adult sitting close to you paraphrasing what the first one was saying.

None of us are immune to sensory overload.

I once had to drive a friend's car in the centre of Paris. He was to drive in front in his wife's car. I had never driven this car before. I had never driven a left-hand drive car before. I had never driven on the right before. Or encountered a roundabout the size of the Plas de la Concorde. Nobody told me that traffic joining the flow had priority!! Worst of all I didn't know the destination and was afraid of being left behind. The anxiety prior to this journey was worse than the grand prix itself. At least my *fight or flight* instincts kicked in once it started. I swore. I waved my hands about. I forgot all the French I knew – apart from the swearwords. I was a gibbering wreck in need of a large cognac by the time we reached chez pal.
Am I normally like that? No. Had I been overextended? Yes.
Overwhelmed? Nearly.
I just couldn't handle the noise, the movement, the need to tweak learnt rules in a novel situation,..

What if it was to be Rome the next day and then Hyde park corner the day after that and so on..... Imagine being taken on this Kafka-esq journey again and again.

What if I had had somebody sitting in the back wittering on at me about 6-figure grid references or quadratic equations.

What neuro-typical adult would not eventually lash out verbally - and even physically.

And whose mental health wouldn't eventually succumb to these pressures.

Their misbehaviour is not wilful. It is a response to being taken to a place that hurts – day after day.

The behaviour represents communication. It is logical that somebody who has a deficit in verbal skills would call upon other means of registering stress and anxiety; other ways of saying 'this is offensive to my innate sense of what is good for me ...STOP it now and get me the hell out of here.

These are **not** wilfully naughty children and they may not respond in standard ways to standard sanctions that assume that they are. The notion of a detention filled my son with dread throughout his school career. Threatening him with one would produce exactly the opposite effect to the intended one. He had to be outside at a certain time to be picked up. That was his schedule. Children with AS are usually desperate to abide by the rules, and fit in, and not be told off.

If a teacher is having a pop at the class in general, they should expect the autistic child to take it very personally. They are not protected by the indifference that a wilful child may display. They really do *want to* get it right. It just takes them much longer to establish *how* to do that.

To add to their woes, as soon as they find out how to survive in one institution, we extract them and make the task ten times harder in a bigger noisier place that has more far more people and rules that ebb and flow depending on the teacher.

The report of the **Irish Task Force on Autism** states -

"The subtlety of its presentation, under-diagnosis and late diagnosis indicate that although identifiable and overt difficult and challenging behaviours sometimes occur within this group, nevertheless such behaviours are not core characteristics of Asperger Syndrome.

This is a crucial thing for both parents and teachers to take on board.

What is being said is that our children's outbursts and difficult behaviour are not an *intrinsic* part of their neurology, but a response to stressors in their immediate environment.

This tends to be backed up by the way most people get a diagnosis: In most cases of Aspergers Syndrome entry into an educational institution is the catalyst for the diagnostic process to start. Concern arises that the individual is not obeying the conventions of the institution.

Some analysts' use this to argue that what we have is a neurological *difference* that *only* becomes a disorder when subjected to stressors such as can be found in a school.

If you sit down in a quiet room with an Aspergers child and discuss his interest in Coronation Street you can envisage an eccentric but coping adult 10 years hence. If you try to teach the same child multiplication tables in a class of thirty, you will conjure up a very different picture. Perhaps, for all our sakes, we should be doing more of the former and less of the latter.

Getting to grips with what the world looks like to an autistic child involves absorbing some new concepts.

'Neurotypicals' (which is what some 'aspies' call non-autistic people) are **Polytropic**. It refers to an ability to handle information from several sources simultaneously. This is something we tend to take for granted. But what if you had profound difficulty prioritising all the information your senses are delivering to your 'central processor'. And consequently were unable to screen out secondary smells, movements, touches. If you were instantly overwhelmed by information coming from more than one source at a time you would be **Monotropic.** Autistic people are thought to be monotropic. It would explain why they avoid eye contact when talking; the less information being taken in, the easier it is to respond. This is why that ghost train was never going to be a favourite haunt for my son.

Impaired **Proprioceptive** ability refers to the difficulty of judging the position of one's body in space. This neurologically based deficit will initially present as difficulty with balance and co-ordination. It makes the playing of socially important ball and chasing games almost impossible. It is partly to blame for the propensity of younger autistic people to invade other people's private body space. With the resulting consequences. And if you talk loudly in a monotone while you are in the nose-to-nose position with somebody you are asking for trouble. Trouble invariably obliges. The demands of body language, posture, gait and dress increase markedly in adolescence.

Being both monotropic and having difficulty with spatial awareness made crossing roads a nightmare for both of us when he was younger. It makes driving a car less likely too – although his recent progress means I'm under some pressure in this respect.

Having difficulties with 'executive function' also makes life much more difficult.

Executive functions are the processes that enable us to take the initiative to do something, plan it, work out an efficient sequence of actions, and sustain that behaviour towards the chosen goal - making adjustments along the way in line with how things are working out. Again these are the types of thought processes that happen almost instantaneously for the rest of us; not so for an autistic person. .

In a school setting an executive dysfunction is at the root of all the organisational difficulties that cause anxiety and friction and frustration. If you watch somebody with AS in a queue to get their lunch you will soon see executive dysfunction at work. Mr Bean is an exponent extraordinaire of executive *dys*function. But it's no laughing matter if you have to put these traits on display to neuro-typical adolescent peers every day. I have seen all sorts of strategies advocated for diminishing organisational difficulties in school but most are unrealistic and underestimate the pace secondary schools operate at. These are skills that can be taught but not 'on the hoof'. That said it isn't as easy off the hoof either. I knew our work on 'taking the initiative' wasn't going so well when he asked me,
" what should I take the initiative on next, Dad'"

Why he might talk loudly in your ear from an inappropriate distance

The fact that he talks loudly to me from a short distance when it's painfully obvious I'm focused on something else, is just one aspect of a language disorder that is also an integral part of autism. It's also bloody annoying. There is a whole set of other rules to abide by; most of which the rest of us seem to know instinctively.

Breaking these *rules* sets you apart from other people.
Apart from using an appropriate eye contact and volume/distance mix
you need to get the tone right if you want to convey the right message. Autistic people tend to talk in a monotone (though my son has added a few variations lately)

And the skill of putting emphasis on particular words to change the meaning of those words does not come naturally to him. Andrew Matthews book **Making Friends** (1990) gives an excellent example of how emphasising different words in a sentence changes the meaning: *I didn't say she stole the money*. Try emphasising each word in turn and see how the meaning changes. What job or social setting doesn't require this skill at some point. Are there situations that would be dangerous without it?

Add to this a propensity to take things that are said literally, echolalia: repeating the words of other people to keep on task, over-formal 'little professor' phrases, and speaking in an accent that differs from your peers despite growing up in the locality.

All in all this represents a serious impediment to being accepted and befriended.

Gaze avoidance whilst attempting to converse is another characteristic of autism. It is possibly an attempt to make it easier to focus on what is being said.

"Look at me when I am talking to you"

is one phrase a teacher might well avoid when talking to an autistic child. Somebody in the 'aspie' community has suggested that if this happens the autistic child should just focus the neuro-typical's nose.

'They will never know the difference'.

My son has learnt to make eye contact with most people.

Unfortunately in adolescence the rules change don't they: Eye contact can convey all sorts of other things which may result in unwarranted responses from the person whose eye you have contacted – especially if you are straining your neck into somebody's face to comply with instructions. Adolescent male conversations often take place sitting side by side in front of a screen with no eye contact expected or welcomed.

Aspies adhere to newly discovered 'rules' with the zeal of a convert; we need to carefully consider the shelf life and importance of the skills we impart.

The wealth of information to be found on the internet.

There is far more information around now than when I was floundering around twelve years ago. Much of this is to be found on the internet. There are some superb websites out there to help autistic people and their parents/teachers. The following are some of the best: www.as-if.org.uk - down to earth, brilliant and comprehensive site created by a young woman with autism; www.TonyAttwood.com - very experienced and empathetic professional; www.autismhelp.info. - v.good; www.nas.org.uk - v.good; www.aspire-irl.com - Asperger's Syndrome support group in Ireland.

Aspire also produce good guidance books for teachers and parents. In one of them they outline some things to remember about children with AS –

- **Motivation** – Competitive motives are absent in the child with AS. This is most apparent in adolescence when other children are desperate to get hold of designer clothes and the latest mobile phone. The fact that my son is just beginning to display avarice represents progress.
- **Imitation** – although an AS child may be able to copy what others do, he finds it difficult to transfer these 'skills' to new situations in an appropriate way: The overarching principle goes unrecognised.
- **Perception** – There will be unexpected responses to situations /stimuli due to misinterpretation of what is going on.
- **Attention** – There will be a narrow and obsessive focus on some detail to the exclusion of the immediate and wider 'picture'.
- **Rigidity of thought** – An AS child will find it difficult to follow a sequence but will adhere to it rigidly once it is absorbed. Problem solving – The child will experience extreme difficulty selecting the right strategy to solve a problem; there is a tendency to seek help immediately following their track record of failure.

The usefulness of the internet doesn't stop there- especially if you are home-educating your child. Given the intensity of their interest in their chosen topic(s) it can be just a case of light the blue touch paper and stand back.

Parents are to blame.

Most teachers think this anyway. And it turns out they are not wrong.

A man called Bruno Bettelheim developed a cosy theory to explain autism. He believed that autism was the mother's fault; for being a *'Refrigerator' Mother*. The blame could be securely left at her door for not bonding properly with her child. It wasn't enough to have to cope with a child displaying eccentric and challenging behaviour, Mum had to accept the behaviour was her fault for the way she was bringing him up.
If they listened to this claptrap, Mothers of autistic children must have been doubly traumatised. I'm surprised they didn't get thrown in ponds to see if they would float or sink!
It has been said that it's a shame when facts spoil a beautiful theory.
Here was a case where a reprehensively ugly theory was, thankfully, spoiled by the facts.

Disempowerment of parents is never a good idea – since these people, once empowered, are the key to a good prognosis.
With the general discreditation of Bettelheim's theory, parents were given a pardon - but it was short-lived.

The consensus of opinion today is that the single biggest factor causing autism is genetic endowment.

So we parents *are* to blame after all.

Studies at Yale University indicate that 30/40% of the immediate family of somebody with Asperger Syndrome will have some degree of 'social difficulties'. Once you know this you tend to re-assess all the endearing little idiosyncrasies you and your relations display.

There is a phrase that is oft trotted out in this context:

'Genes load the gun but environment pulls the trigger.'

This begs the question as to *what* environmental factors might be at work?

As in the case of the 'remedies' the triggers are many, varied and largely unproven. If there was a runner-up to genes in the causation stakes it would be 'trauma at birth'. Others point to: vaccines; food intolerances; toxins; infections during pregnancy. This is not an exhaustive list.

In Sean's case I look at the list of triggers and reflect that it could have been all or any of these factors. Got that. Did that. Experienced that. Certainly, on reflection, the genetic argument seems a strong one. If I say more I will get even less Christmas cards than usual.

Whilst the origin of the condition is very important it is of academic interest to a diagnosed individual - food intolerance being the obvious exception.

As the Solution Focused therapists point out

' knowledge is not the same as change'.

So, with apologies to vegetarians, 'it's time to stop weighing the pig and time to start fattening it.' The research will go on, but in the mean time it is more important to focus on how we alleviate its adverse impact on current generations.

There is no 'silver bullet' for Autism.

And we really should think twice about shooting children anyway. This horrible phrase sums up all that is bad about interventions designed to 'fix' our children. It is tantamount to wishing we could have a different child. There are days when the most saintly parent might want things to be a bit easier. But that isn't the same as wishing away a child you have come to know and love. The target should be that chunk of the 'difference' that will cause him pain now and in the future. That said, as parents it's only natural to want to do *something*.

But formulating therapies to help children at the Asperger end of the autistic spectrum is a young 'science' and, short of genetic modification,
is never going to be an exact one. There are too many variables and every child is different.
There *is* a near consensus (not 100%) that there *is* no such thing as a 'silver bullet'. But parents are confronted with a bewildering range of alternative weaponry to at least wound the beast.

The list includes established therapies such as occupational and speech therapy. Most people would be rightly keen to access more of these proven interventions.
But many 'new' interventions have been developed.
Each of them purporting to be the best use of our time energy - and often our money.
Given time, energy, and money are in scarce supply it would be good to have some idea of what works best.

Which approach confers most desirable change per minute /joule / euro?

The most comprehensive and dispassionate assessment I have found is in **The Report of the Task Force on Autism published by the Dept. of Education and Science in Ireland.**

In 2001 they had no research on which to evaluate the **Son Rise** approach which does, they say, have the advantage of empowering parents who often feel 'heard' for the first time.

The following were positively reported on **or** the jury was still out but with good anecdotal feedback:

Sensory Integration Therapy;

Vitamin Therapy (B6 and Magnesium);

Gluten and Casein free diet programmes;

the Higashi approach;

Floor Time (Stanley Greenspan M.D.).

Two others are singled out for mention, with their usefulness more substantiated by empirical evidence.

They are **ABA – Applied Behavioural Analysis** and

TEACCH – The Treatment and Education of Autistic and Communication Handicapped Children.

Unfortunately the efficacy of these two interventions seems to be less clear cut for those on the Asperger part of the spectrum.

In particular the Task Force point out that the frequent repetitive drills have only been tested with younger children operating more towards the 'classic' end of the spectrum. The ABA approach does tend to see behaviours as 'wilful' and some children may be 'over-stressed' by the approach. But anecdotally some parents swear it has transformed their children.

The reservation with TEACCH is that its emphasis on visual clues; the task force concluded that it

". may be of limited use to high functioning students ...who can talk."

It may be that subsequent research has clarified the options.

I don't have the knowledge or the arrogance to rule anything in or out: Even if I had the benefit of his early years again I am still unsure about what I would do beyond the occupational and speech therapy.

Or whether I would anything.

The options seem to divide up into developing skills to bear down on dysfunctional behaviours or focusing on where the child is and taking it from there.

There is anecdotal evidence to make both approaches

attractive, but if I had to jump in one direction it would be probably be in line with the thinking of John W. Gardener who said

"If you have some respect for people as they are you can be more effective in helping them to become better than they are."

Knowing what I know now I would therefore be drawn towards the Son-Rise or Floor Time programmes.

If I had the old Sierra days back, I would sit in the car and talk about the cassette player he was playing with as if it were the most natural thing to do. He wouldn't know I was in *his* world only to entice him back into mine. *(I'm* not averse to a bit of deception. I used to tell the pupils in my 'inclusion unit' that I was a cousin of Mick Foley – the giant American wrestler.)

I also have a great deal of empathy towards columnist Charlotte Moore's approach since it's basically what I have done over the years. Charlotte has two children with ASDs.

"I am convinced that one must lay siege to an autistic child. There is no cure for autism. There is no 'normal' child screaming to get out. It is in everyone's best interests to modify their less acceptable behaviours. The sooner the siege begins the greater the results will be."

Charlotte Moore's siege might also be viewed as the belligerent wing of

Cognitive **Behaviour Therapy**. (CBT). Assuming a parent can judge when to sally forth and when to retreat since they know their child best.

It is perfectly possible to respect a child but disrespect the autistic trait that will cause them hurt if it remains active. Always bearing in mind that time may be the best siege engine in our armoury.

Two aspects of CBT appeal to me in particular: Firstly, as an Economics teacher I have inbuilt intolerance for illogical statements based on dodgy facts and wonky analysis.
Therefore I haven't been able to help myself waging a war of attrition on his eccentric reasoning. I know this needs to be taken on.
The second appealing skill from CBT is the installation of strategies to combat negative feelings. If he feels down now he will go and have a dance to some music, or have a bounce on the trampoline, or maybe take himself out for a game of darts and a pot of tea.

JM Keynes said,

'If the facts change I change my mind ...what do you do?

I *would* change my mind if the intensive behavioural programmes were proven to work. But the evidence simply isn't there yet to allow a full appraisal to be made. It's very early days for 'AS'.

Then again if it's on offer locally   - why not give it a lash.
If it's stressful – ditch it.

It's possible that the 'Hawthorne effect' may come into play. The 'Hawthorne' effect refers to the rewards reaped from just paying close attention to a person. There *is* considerable evidence that 'clients' in therapy benefit, not so much from what approach is being used, but from a good relationship with their therapist, so ...

It's not what you do - it's the way that you do it?

So unless the practitioner is insensitive or the process is stressful it would take a braver parent than me to turn anything down flat.

The big exception for me being drug therapy; the combination of pharmaceuticals and immature neurology involves uncharted risks.

I would also *still* be a bit suspicious of interventions that have to implemented precisely as their authors dictate,

x number of hours, A before B. unless this then that....

as if a particular fixed sequence was appropriate for every individual in every circumstance.

In this less than altruistic world some people are more interested in what is in your pocket than what is in your child's head.

Perhaps improvements are more to do with what you *stop* doing than what you *start* doing: I was told of a couple in Cork.

After the usual frustrations with the 'system they have 'opted out'.

All that energy that was applied to fighting for resources and interventions now goes into quality time with their child.

They go fishing together.

If I had my time again I would worry less and do more 'Fishing boat therapy'.

This sort of attitude may horrify those with a mindset that is now screaming ' but what about SCHOOL!!!

But ...what about it!

If time is chipping away at the deficits- like a glacier carving out a valley, the bottom line is not to do anything that stops the process or slows it down or reverses it.

And that includes 'school'.

School doesn't work for everybody.

Anyway.

How *did* we get into a situation where inculcating exam skills became the core remedy for atypical neurology?

Maybe we should 'Free the Omega 3'

It seems likely that some kind of dietary intervention will eventually be shown to be helpful.
Again it requires a zeal and a discipline that I couldn't muster without the firmest of evidence. .
I would cease to function as a useful parent if I had to deliver him a gluten-free and casein-free diet.
He has difficulty getting his muscles to co-operate in swallowing tablets, so milk with added Omega 3 has been our main nod in the direction of dietary supplements. Though orange flavoured chewy Omega 3 has just appeared on the supermarket shelves. I worry that stronger doses of fish oil may deliver more dioxins than an eastern European election, but the highly respected Madeleine Portwood (University of Durham guru on Dyspraxia) is an impressive advocate of this approach.

The issue for me is how you screen out the maturation process etc from the distinct benefits of any single intervention. In short:

How do you embrace the fish oil saleswomen whilst avoiding the snake oil salesmen?

Until the science hardens up, I'd be more sure of what **NOT** to do.

Eastern European Gymnastics Coach (1960) Syndrome

(Oh no.. not another bloody syndrome!)

This syndrome arises when an unholy alliance of pushy parents and subject fundamentalist teachers contrive to make life hell for the child. All in pursuit of some 'gold standard' that says more about their aspirations than it does about the well-being of the child. It's thankfully rare. More often than not one side is trying to get the other side to be a bit less dogmatic and rigid.

Teachers need to listen to parents. Even if they are a pain in the bottom. And just thank your god that you don't have their battles to fight. The prime duty of a parent is to protect their child from harm.
To protect that vulnerable individual from situations and people who could hurt it. That **must** include people and individuals who would harm him **unintentionally** - through negligence or ignorance or arrogance.
The list of potential culprits includes the state, bureaucrats and the medical profession. **And teachers!** Deference is cowardice.
This is **their** child. He doesn't belong to the CBI or the State or the School. Their children are likely to have to cope for many years without them.
If they leave them a legacy of low self-esteem they leave them worse than nothing. .
So forgive them if they *are* a pain in the bottom.
They can't allow their child to experience failure as a daily diet - just because a transient institution has been forced to adopt a particularly narrow definition of *success.*

If, however, it is the parents who are pushing the child too hard an empathetic and informed teacher is the best ally the child can have.
Their mental health may depend on **your** timely intervention .

Perception is all important.

When they built the first skyscrapers the residents complained that the lifts were too slow. The Otis lift company installed mirrors in the lifts and the complaints.. went down. Sometimes the fundamentals can't be changed so we have to find a way of living with them.

What we tell them about themselves and what they tell themselves about themselves is so important .The future can look *ok* because it is a unique future; their future. If he doesn't get 5 good GCSE's. If he doesn't get married. If he doesn't work full-time. If his income is modest - and statistically these are the most likely outcomes – his is still a life with equal validity to any pope or president.

It is illogical for his education or his self-worth to be driven by the narrow criterion for success that politicians have foisted on schools.

My son will cope as an adult if he has the right frame of mind and appropriate skills. But I *can't* give him this frame of mind if a teacher is taking this perspective away from him on a daily basis.

Neither can I give him this perspective if I haven't developed it myself.

Ruble and Dalrymple (1996) put it very nicely this way:

Defining outcome as the relationship between an individual's challenges and strengths, environmental stressors and supports, and other people's perceptions of competence and self-perceptions of quality of life is more likely to yield a better combination of predictor variables than simply measures of IQ and language.

A positive self-perception is the bedrock on which his quality of life will be determined.

If he *is* less likely to get a job he will be 'time-rich'.

f he isn't going to get married - relish the tranquillity of being a singleton.

If he can't drive a car, to think of the health, environmental and financial benefits.

If he doesn't do that well in your algebra test ...so what?

To what extent do the problems *still* exist if we take the bog-standard life objectives away.

To what extent should we be setting them up for *failure* in relation to conventional criteria.

To what extent does a different value system diminish the need to 'fix' the individual?

If we transmit the notion that only gregariousness, exam success, a job, material wealth, marriage and offspring constitute 'success' then we immediately turn many autistic people into failures.

We need to avoid invalidating whole lives because the blinkers are on and superficiality reigns. In surveys of post Celtic-tiger Ireland people often say they are *less* happy than they were in less materialistic times. One in three people in London live alone. Expectations of fulfilment in the arms of another are often thwarted. Many people dislike their jobs and only do them to earn money.

We *all* want to feel useful and we *all* want to be accepted, so enabling autistic people to perceive themselves as 'useful' is very important.

We have no right to subject them to damaging levels of frustration and anxiety in pursuit of some *ideal* lifestyle that the rest of us rarely attain anyway.

If we shift the mindset away from a conventional path to 'success', all concerned benefit.

94

One of the key ingredients for contentment is **gratitude** for what you have.
If we transmit a daily message of their 'failure' for years on end *they* will inevitably suffer, and so will we.

Professor Katarina Tomasevski of Lund University, Sweden has warned of the dangers of overtesting in English schools. Asking whether the government was seeking to emulate Singapore, where in a poll of 10-12 year olds, pupils said they were more worried about failing their exams than their parents dying.

Anxiety is something that comes as standard with AS. They need more of it like they need another hole in the head.

For the ultimate perception tweaker log on to www.nas.com/downsyn/holland

Thank you Emily Pearl Kingsley. Wow!

'Success' for children with AS merits a wider definition than is currently the case.

Success is a subjective concept but some respected commentators are confident enough to turn it into an objective one.

"For the majority of high functioning children with autism, their chances of living a full and independent life will be dependent on whether they are able to obtain academic qualifications at school, which will in turn allow them to progress to further education and eventually a job. With few exceptions the only way in which this can be achieved will be by attending a mainstream school."
Patricia Howlin in Autism: Preparing for Adulthood.

I think the above position is open to question:
Do 'academic qualifications' confer much needed life skills;
who exactly has the right to define what a '*full*' life might consist of;
what if this process increases stress and the risk of mental illness?

I think we should be very careful not to impose a set of criteria which, if unfulfilled, constitute 'failure'. That smacks of arrogance.

The conventional position is a powerful magnet though, and is much trumpeted on this side of the Irish Sea too:

"The importance of education for the development of the individual's potential cannot be overestimated and keeping the AS/HFA child at school for as long as possible should be the main focus of professional interventions"(SWAHB 2001)

On the contrary, I think it can *easily* be overestimated: Keeping a child in a stressful environment with an inappropriate curriculum 'for as long as possible' is plain daft.

Is it not simplistic in the extreme to base educational provision for an individual on generalisations that pre-judge the needs of that individual.

Especially when there is a huge amount of anecdotal evidence to indicate the risk being taken with a child's self-esteem and mental health.
Their chances of living '*a full and independent life*' are hardly enhanced if a person ends up as a guinea pig for the latest anti-psychotic drugs or in an under-funded mental hospital.

For many adolescents and young adults too much time spent focused on their difficulties may have an adverse effects on their strengths.

There is an apocryphal tale about a Chinese table tennis coach. He was interviewed as he basked in the reflective glory of his all-conquering team. When asked about the key to their success his response was,

I ask the players to concentrate on their strengths.

The next question concerned what he did about their weaknesses.

His response,

I do nothing about their weaknesses.

I spent the first twelve years of my son's life coming at things from exactly the opposite direction. So did most other adults he encountered.

What message were we transmitting.

How much damage did we do?

The education systems in these islands require specialisation to be put off until the age of 16/18. Children who opt out before this age are increasingly viewed as failures .Yet there are many children – and not just those on the autistic spectrum - who would benefit from individualised paths from a much earlier age.

This applies to many autistic adolescents whose portfolio of skills/interests contains a passion that can be nurtured vocationally.

Too often – and this applies to 'neuro-typical' teenagers too – their enthusiasm for a particular pursuit is glossed over or even derided and discouraged.

The *system* scoffs at their passions as a distraction and demands that they be dragged back to a conventional curriculum.

This is taken to ridiculous lengths sometimes: There is minor kudos in the English exam league tables for disadvantaged schools **if** they get each child at least ONE exam pass *regardless of the grade*!

Much sweat and tears goes into this quest regardless of the fact it cuts no ice for the child in the labour market.

I remember one young man who was continuously dragged off his uncle's fruit stall, where he was learning his family's trade, to sit in a classroom that he hated and disrupted. This defies common sense.

Getting them through at least one exam is a purely institutional objective, whilst nurturing their passion may be the key to unlocking self-esteem and perhaps even a vocation.

My son has always had a real interest in History.

He is noticeably more adept at manipulating numbers when they appear in a historical context. This has now morphed into a passion for genealogy and his own website and small business.

Did I mention this elsewhere? Oh well, what harm …
www.irishroots-census.com.

I think we need to be more like the Chinese tennis coach. People with AS have their passions. Let's systematically engage with those passions. Let's wait in the long grass for one to arise – and then leap on it with relish.
Watch their self-esteem barometer rising when we do.

Who would have thought that a book about a dead dog would raise awareness of AS.

Mark Haddon has done a great profile-raising job for Aspergers Syndrome, with his best-selling novel **'The curious incident of the dog in the night-time'**. The story has a central character who operates on the high functioning segment of the autistic spectrum. Not since Dustin Hoffman's rainman has a fictional character impacted on the global perception of autism to this extent. I have no doubt that Christopher is out there somewhere. I'm still not entirely sure - given his academic profile - just how he managed to stay out of a mainstream school. Was his Dad aware of the things I've only just copped onto? Or had he kicked his reception teacher at the mainstream primary school? Christopher is not exactly thrilled to bits with his special school placement.

This would tie in with the notion that a placement in a low cognitive functioning environment is less than appropriate.

In **Inclusion and Autism: Is it working?** Barnard Prior and Potter note

'that parents are no happier with generic special schools (without autism specific provision) than they are with mainstream with some learning support. Children with autism and Asperger Syndrome have uneven abilities and it may not be appropriate for them to be in a setting for children with learning disabilities where it is assumed that abilities are equal across a range of subjects.

Christopher was particularly unlucky to meet a Principal who would argue the toss over his early entry for his Maths A level. Most headteachers would be falling over themselves to help and, far from hindering the process, they would celebrate the child's ability and set about facilitating it.

Not to mention getting the local media in pronto.

Mark Haddon's 'Christopher John Francis Boone' has a 'Swiss cheese' set of skills and deficits. Just like two Swiss cheeses never have holes in the same place, my son has a portfolio of abilities that differs markedly from CJF Boone. My son would never thump a policeman or enjoy his subsequent sojourn in a police cell. Unlike Christopher, he sleeps very well; in this respect he is in the minority I think. He *does* have a nice sense of humour and enjoys some kinds of jokes. Christopher intends doing a maths degree and knows every prime number up to 7,507; my son has significant difficulty with numbers outside a historical context.

I have taught my son to tell fibs in delicate social situations whilst Christopher tells it how it is, warts and all. My son's fine motor skills are slightly impaired - the construction of an airfix model would not be his forte.

There are of course many traits that they do share, but the differences are such that they would require markedly different interventions. Generic training on autism and Aspergers syndrome has its place but in order to be of real use to a child you have to first know that child.

Even when you do, there is a tendency to focus almost exclusively on their weaknesses. In so far as it stops somebody punching policemen I accept it has to be a bit of a priority.

So not only is every autistic child different to the next, but what needs to be addressed first will differ.

Templates do not really exist.

It calls for pragmatic rather than dogmatic thinking and actions.

All of which is a complete nightmare for a secondary school teacher who has thirty minutes 'quality time' with thirty children, before the next thirty trot in. The mindset in a conventional educational setting is all about filling gaps in a pre-determined set of skills. It rarely provides the opportunity to develop the quirky attributes to be found in young autistic people.

'The Incidents in a day of the Curious Child in the Mainstream '

For a child that does end up in a mainstream secondary school most days can be a bit of an assault course e.g. **8.30**: Get dropped off at school in the car. (Two visual-spatially exacting roads to cross **or** the school bus aka the narrow river crossing for Wildebeest on a David Attenborough wildlife special.). **8.40**: Get called 'spaz' by two older boys while waiting for doors to open. **8.45**: Mild panic in the movement towards doors - push somebody. Get told off by teacher on the door. **8.50**: Get pushed out of form queue whilst waiting for form tutor. Two girls from 'circle of friends' come to the rescue. Consequently called *gay boy* by class **Predator. 8.55**: Thinking about incident at door. Indignation wells up. Decide to tell form tutor. Mention predator whilst at it. Big sigh and raised eyebrows from teacher. (What does that mean?) Dirty look from **Predator.** (Learnt that one. Gulp!) **9.00**: Get prize in assembly for collecting most old stamps for Christmas appeal. Get big round of applause that goes on *slightly* too long from some p-takers at the back. Make formal acceptance speech! **9.10**: Join melee en route to first lesson ...P. E. - Take too long to change. Get bellowed at by teacher as part of tardy group. Not personal but take it as such. Rounders – teacher lets P.E. student take half the class.. student appoints two captains for the teams. Get picked last. Get confused when told to drop the bat when running to first base. PE student shouts 'hey spaceman'. Boys laugh. Girls offer T.L.C. **10.18:** Late for maths lesson and dishevelled. Supply teacher is struggling to start the lesson. Try to explain you have permission to go to Head of Year if there is a supply teacher. Get told to sit down. **Predator** is in this maths set. He starts to flick paper and issue dire warnings about break-time. Getting very agitated and vocal. Learning assistant turns up in nick of time. Get to go with her to learning support area. Very wound up and anxious about break-time. Calm down after chat. No maths done. **11.10**: Breaktime. Stick close to break duty teacher asking her 101 questions about her car. Try to get can out of drinks machine but get totally flustered when it doesn't deliver. Throw a tantrum that has others laughing. Get even more wound up. Kick machine. Get sent to stand outside staffroom. Next to **Predator!** Big sigh from the teacher that opens the staffroom door. Try to explain what's happened. Get totally frustrated when not allowed to. Sent to next lesson when the bell goes. **11.30:** Geography. Totally distracted. Going over the events of the morning in head. Six figure grid references difficult and of little interest. 'Subject fundamentalist' teacher not impressed. Put outside the room for refusing to put pen to paper. Deputy head arrives – get to go to his room to work. Have a good chat. Calm down a bit. Get to stay until lunchtime. **12.30: Lunch-time ...**most stressful bit of the day. Queue up for Dining room. Get pushed out of queue. Told to go to the back by unknown teacher. Have difficulty with tray and plates and drink. Eat alone. Go to Library to help out. Older kids have got all the best jobs. Try to negotiate by pointing out today's rota. They take no notice. Storm off. Go outside...get invited to play game – have rules of pitch n toss explained - lose money at pitch n toss. Walk through a game of football. Get called names. Stand near door ready to go in. **1.20:** Afternoon registration. Explain electronic registration machine to Form Tutor. Get big thank you 1.30: Computing. Try to explain electronic registration to computer teacher. Get told off. Learning Support Teacher sits in. Other children in pairs. Have a good chat to LST about his car. Haven't done homework! Didn't have time to write it down when support teacher was absent last time. 15 minute detention. Can't do detentions because Dad comes at a certain time in the car. Get very agitated and vocal. Support teacher tells computer teacher to recall that there was a 'memo' a month ago: Detention withdrawn. Other detainees *not* impressed. Get to leave lesson early to avoid corridor maelstrom. **2.30:** History. Favourite lesson. Sit at the front and answer every question. Even ones that haven't been asked yet! No learning support. Sense of independence. A relatively good day finishes at **3.30**.

Some days are nowhere near as good.

They can fall at the first hurdle and the rest of the day is little more than a fire-fighting exercise.

Go home knackered and maybe in tears… that's just the teachers.

The days that *do* go 'ok' are the ones where the 'people factors' outweighs the 'institutional factors'. My son had a brilliant support teacher who still keeps in touch with him. People like her are worth their weight in gold.

But some days it's a bit like a snowball gathering pace on a hill – with stressors hitting the child at a rate that cannot be absorbed or ameliorated by the best of strategies or people.

These are the days that do damage.

If – after strategy 'make-overs' have been tried - there is still an increasing incidence of such days more drastic steps must be taken.

Possibly big ones ….out the gate and up the gangway at Holyhead.

If we know they are pre-disposed to Depression then we need to be proactive in heading it off.

The Kerry Mental Health Association points out in its Spring '04 newsletter that

" Mental Health is far more than the absence of mental illness. "

They go on to emphasise three contributory factors in determining mental health:
1) How you feel about yourself
2) How you feel about other people
3) How you are able to meet the demands of life

They go on to sub-divide these key factors into specific attitudes.

Mentally healthy people feel good about themselves. They:

- are not overwhelmed by their own emotions – fears, anger, worries;
- take disappointments in their stride;
- have a tolerant easy going disposition and can laugh at themselves;
- Neither underestimate or overestimate their abilities;
- can accept their own shortcomings;
- take pleasure in simple everyday things

If you compare these desirable characteristics to the typical presentation in Asperger-type autism you start to see fertile ground for mental health problems.

It doesn't stop there.

Mentally healthy people also feel comfortable with other people.

- They are able to love and consider the interests of others;
- have personal relationships that are satisfying and lasting;
- like and trust others;
- feel they are part of a group.

Again if we audit this second batch of characteristics with autism in mind you really couldn't get more of a mis-match. Their inter-personal skills deficit militates against peace of mind.

Finally, mentally healthy people are able to meet the demands of life, they:

- do something about their problems as they arise;
- shape their environment whenever possible;
- they adjust to it whenever necessary;
- plan ahead and do not fear the future;
- welcome new experiences and ideas.

The level of anxiety that many autistic people experience and the frustrating lack of 'executive' skills they live with means these attitudes/skills are never innate.

If most of these supportive attitudes and skills are absent in autistic people the propensity to suffer mental health problems is established.

It makes little sense to send this vulnerable individual into an environment full of stressors. Either we put the attributes in place or we steer clear of overtaxing situations. Or a bit of both.

Putting these attributes in place **is** possible but it requires *explicit* teaching of the attributes and a good deal of time; time that is currently devoted to much less important things.

There seems to be a number of different phases.

There seems to be a fairly typical roller coaster for children and their parents.
Phase 1 is recognising that our child is 'different'.

In **Phase 2** the difference is highlighted by their inability to conform to institutional norms in the nursery/ reception class / early primary years.

Phase 3 involves partial accommodation of the 'difference' by initially bemused teachers and peers.

This relative *'calm before the storm'* occurs in the middle primary school years. Places are found in the school nativity play, everybody cheers his relative success on sports day. Teachers 'up-skill' and pass on strategies as our child moves through the school. Despite the self-interested intrusion of politicians in the curriculum, primary schools are still not *institutionally exclusive* in the way that secondary schools are. The short lines of communication and the holistic flexibility of primary schools can be a godsend Not to make light of all the problems that do arise, but this can be a time to relish. This eye of the storm is a very dangerous time though because it induces a complacency that is inappropriate; it can become all too easy to underestimate the scale of the task ahead at this point.

Phase 4 coincides with the onset of adolescence in an increasingly hostile environment. Self-awareness increases and self-esteem decreases. Stress levels increase and peer support decreases. Fatigue and exasperation levels increase on both sides of the teacher's desk. Disaffection, disruption, and possibly depression kick in.

The trick is obviously ....to avoid Phase 4.

Milestones can become millstones.

Slavish adherence to conventional rites of passage is inappropriate if a child has unconventional neurology. We need to embrace a time-scale for their development that is outside the norm. This may be at odds with the demands of 'school'.

"Many people with AS/HFA are late reaching maturity and should be given every opportunity to develop at their own pace with the continuing provision of education/therapeutic support…. unaided many of this group may deteriorate to a point where they may need long term residential/psychiatric care at the expense of their potential abilities and at considerable cost to the state. …This is a vulnerable high-risk group in urgent need of help."
The Report of the Irish Task Force on Autism 2000

From the time they fail their 18-month MOT we start to play an unwinnable game of catch-up. The *system* takes over and helps us try to achieve those missed 'milestones' and then there are new rites of passage to be observed: At the nursery. At school. At 16. At 18. At college. At work. Marriage. Children. Buying a house.

But a diagnosis of AS requires a mindset devoid of time-bonded milestones - lest they become millstones around our children's necks. It isn't easy to step back and play the 'long game' but it is important not to get swept along in the rush because we are afraid to be different.

Taking a still developing child off a conventional path and going on a different journey is not an easy thing to do.

But there **will** be casualties if they are pushed through at a pace that does not suit.

For some children 'sitting out' the first few years of second-level education could represent better 'gap years' than waiting until they are 18 or 21.

Different feet require different shoes.

If we do not recognize, accept and act on their different neurology there are implications e.g.

'Self-esteem will become exceptionally low'

– so states the **aspire** guidance booklet for teachers.

They are talking about teenagers… *our* teenagers.
This is a truly frightening statement in its apparent inevitability.

As if we should, for one minute, countenance allowing this to happen!

To enforce attendance in an environment where failure is a daily experience is to render irrevocable damage. Even if my child *were* academically gifted I would not trade wealth for health. Because if you lose the latter you will soon lose the former; it is fools gold that is being dug for. With self-esteem goes any sense of worth and acceptance. Would it not be better to drip feed challenges that matter in an environment where sensory and linguistic deficits are given time to diminish. Examinations can be taken at any age. Jobs can be found when the time is right. You can get married when you are 50.

The role of parents in warding off meltdown of self-esteem is crucial. It is highlighted by Rebecca Moyes,

" A high percentage of adolescents with AS experience depression when they feel they are not accepted by peers and society in general.
Home may be the only place where a child feels accepted."

Having his friends in a circle might make him dizzy.

In order to survive in the 'mainstream' most parents have to 'go public' about their child's disability. Keeping 'it' under wraps rules out 'circles of friends' for one thing. But this is no easy decision; would you want your medical details given out to all your colleagues?

Bearing in mind the part the chosen 'environment' has to play in *creating* the problems, there has to be a bit of mangled logic in this somewhere.

First we place them in an institution that induces autistic behaviour and highlights their difference. Then we try to compensate for that outcome by employing their adolescent peers to 'look after them'.

This is a fairly high price to pay for attending the institution.

Anecdotal evidence indicates that it is often the girls in the class who will be most diligent in encircling their designated 'friend'.

For a boy this does nothing for his already paltry corridor-cred.

It can and does leave him open to taunts about his sexuality.

For the children that make up the circle there is no doubt a measure of personal development.

This, and the diminished likelihood of *physical* bullying, seem to be the main attributes.

My son was very aware that it was an artificial construct.

He quite liked it nevertheless - even though none of 'the circle' sought to extend this relationship outside school hours.

I'm sure there are instances where the 'chemistry' and the environment are such that the benefits are greater. Every child and situation is unique.

That said, as is the case with so many laudable interventions, there is a need to envisage how it will operate at the child's eye level.

Looking back it now seems like a very small sticking plaster on a wound that was getting bigger by the day.

Dyscalculia fundamentally changes the cost-benefit balance of mainstream schooling.

My son has significant difficulties with numbers. Unless they are presented in the form of dates. I re-trained as a maths teacher partly because I felt inadequate when it came to helping him cope with this deficit, and I felt guilty for losing my rag with him - when he couldn't cope with basic sums homework and I couldn't fathom what the problem was.

Maths teachers are in short supply.

The Ofsted inspector at the school where I was 'on supply' said I was 'good' and asked what it would take for me to stay on at the school.

I told him I would stay on at the school as long as people like him didn't – which would happen if the school 'failed' its inspection.

It didn't thanks to - its inspirational Headteacher - my good friend, Michael Buczynski RIP. A Head and a ball-boy at Old Trafford in the same lifetime. I'm not jealous - honest.

I learnt a lot about teaching sums to less able children in that school.
That said Dyscalculia is another syndrome that the average teacher will raise their eyebrows to. It is not a term that circulates freely – even within maths departments.

And yet, for every maths prodigy on the autistic spectrum there is another autistic child whose neurological portfolio includes a number deficit that is significantly out of kilter with their other cognitive skills.

This may be due to a combination of difficulties such as language processing, difficulties with sequencing, visual spatial problems, transference of skills/knowledge to new contexts, motor skill deficits, and high levels of anxiety – with the latter being possibly cause as well as effect.

Whatever the root causes the impact is highly significant. As a child moves up the years in a mainstream secondary school there is an inbuilt assumption in non-maths lessons that numerical skills are developing relatively normally.
If this is *not* the case then access to the curriculum is effectively denied. Scarcely a subject at GCSE/Junior Cert does not require an ability to juggle with numbers. Certainly grades that 'open doors' are unattainable.
Most third level courses insist on a basic mathematical attainment in any case. The lucrative careers of engineering and computing so beloved of numerically able autistic people are off the agenda.

An autistic child who is also dyscalculic therefore has the intolerable burden of 'failing' academically **and** socially **and** on the sports-field.

I believe that the presence of a significant numerical deficit in an autistic child is a key determinant of the best way forward.

It swings the balance heavily *against* the pursuit of a conventional post-primary education. There has to be a bloody good reason for subjecting an autistic child to a mainstream secondary experience. Take away exam 'success' and you have an option that involves potentially huge costs and few benefits beyond the befriending a handful of supportive adults.

When we first jumped ship to 'home school ', I started off formally trying to impart 'academic' maths skills. I found it surprisingly difficult to abandon fractions and percentages et al. Two years ago I took a step back and finally realised the futility of my approach. I took the pressure off. Anxiety levels went down. Confidence levels went up. Bit like when I stopped trying to teach him to ride that bike. These days we do our sums in the same context as we practise life skills. He is much improved.

For a dyscalculic child, there is insufficient on offer in the mainstream to warrant the taking of any risks. I just wish that somebody had spelt this out to me seven years ago. It is testimony to the pull to be 'normal' that I didn't work it out for myself; it seems so painfully obvious now.

'Common sense takes a back seat when desire takes the wheel'.

My son came out with this beauty when I explained the difficulty of getting a dog in our current circumstances i.e. renting a house. I *think* it's original!!
We got the dog anyway!

It applies equally well to my response, seven years ago, when I was told he was '*able*' enough to go to a mainstream secondary school. The final review meeting in primary school is possibly the most important meeting the parent of an autistic child will ever attend. Christopher John Francis Boone of dog in the night-time fame, is fairly scathing about economists who are "are not real scientists."
But whilst economics will never be a pure science it does have its uses.
Weighing up the costs and benefits of a project can help to deliver better decisions. The project in question being the education of an autistic child in a mainstream secondary school.
There are benefits. There are costs.
Given that verbal autistic children are increasingly being placed in mainstream schools presumably you would think it has been established that the benefits outweigh the costs.

In reality the decision is rarely subject to anything approaching the rigour of cost-benefit analysis. Given the possible implications for the individual it should be. We are talking about possibly putting somebody's mental health in jeopardy.

But given that parents do **not** have all the information at their disposal, and face an apparently confident and professional consensus to 'mainstream', the outcome is understandable.
Most parents, myself included, sieze the verdict with glee.
It is a 'trophy' to relish after all the worries over the years.
All the Economics training - and I just glossed over the possible downside.
No pertinent questions from me that day.
Too happy.
Too scared of rocking the boat. Mainstream here we go!

I grew up next door to the old Manchester United training ground in Salford.

I would therefore be disinclined to line up alongside an Arsenal fan on too many issues - but Nick Hornby talking on radio 4, 22.10.04 brought up parental egos as a factor in this decision making process,

"Parents of autistic children have to ask themselves. why do you want to send your child to a mainstream school …is it for the child's benefit or for YOUR benefit."?

Nick Hornby   (who also has a child who is autistic.)

The truth is that nobody actually knows how things will work out for the mainstreamed child in years to come. But the process cannot just take the benefits as read, and the costs as acceptable and surmountable.

Not when those costs are potentially so great.

And when the criteria for placement are exclusively academic.

Having an excellent memory for facts has a downside.

He has excellent long-term recall of detail.

In years to come he will be sought after by pub quiz teams; a good way to make friends.

This attribute on its own should, however, **never ever** have sufficient weight on its own to have a mainstream placement deemed appropriate.

Too often specialist provision never comes onto the table as an option because **recall** is still the skill most tested in the mainstream.

Their comparative advantage often confers on them the 'little professor' status that Asperger referred to.

Notwithstanding the additional intellectual requirements of a secondary school curriculum. Or the huge social deficit that will be a major factor throughout those years. There is no way that this splinter skill should hold sway in the placement decision.

It should be seen as an indicator of eccentric development.

As such it is more likely to indicate propensity to be bullied rather than ability to cope and flourish.

Parents and teachers can employ lots of devices to make life easier and better.

S.E.W. applies every morning. Shower. Exercise. Work. This is a structure to the early part of the day that works for us. The shower and the exercise are both designed to *fire up* his brain chemistry - a phrase borrowed from a local chiropractor - so that what comes after is more productive.

Our routine has been a lot more laid back than the mad rush to get to school but we still needed a structure.

STT simply stands for Stop – Think – Talk. It (sometimes) helps him to avoid saying silly things that he will regret as soon as they are out, and subsequently spend 3 days berating himself for.

'Cows in the field' is a good one. If you lie down perfectly still in a cow field and close your eyes you will soon be surrounded by curious cows looking down at you. Many young people with AS crave social interaction and try too hard to get it. This has the opposite effect and drives people away; nobody enjoys having their personal space invaded so they can be subjected to a loud monologue. My son has learnt to sit, saying nothing, and wait for others to make the first move. It works … more often than not.

Going to the **same** shops and restaurants and bank – asking for the same drinks – talking to the same people: Getting known in the community. Sharing the time of day, talking about the weather. These things matter but they have to be taught.

In line with the objective of making him more independent he now plans out his week's work on paper – I intervene now only when asked.

Lifts to the library or the beach for a walk. Increasingly he will sort his own transport out. He keeps a diary for reflecting on how things have gone – the general tone of his inputs is very positive.

There are lots of devices 'out there' to assist children survive the obstacle course of school. They no doubt help but I think the real solution is a structural one.

So near and yet ...

The noble efforts of the unit in Sheffield mentioned earlier are honestly outlined in the book **Access and Inclusion for children with Autistic Spectrum Disorders: Matthew Hemondshalgh and Christine Breakey.**

At one point the authors note teething problems for the unit.

Early on in the year.. I noted that the physical environment was having a large effect on our student's ability to cope with their learning environment.... a noisy crowded busy overheated environment could cause over-stimulation and excitement...groups of students gathering at the entrances caused stress...moving around the college was both over-stimulating and stressful.

In the light of this, many would advocate a learning situation far from the madding crowd: Home Education is the ultimate environmental 'fix'.
If the main reason for risking a mainstream placement is access to specialist teaching perhaps the solution involves having access to this provision at a time when there are less people around.
Perhaps on a one-to-one or small group basis in twilight lessons.
If teachers had their conventional teaching load lightened some would agree to do this.
I would have done it.

Work is a four letter word.

The instinct to have our offspring *prosper* must run very deep in us.
With the means to that end involving replication of our own progress; using the institutions and devices we grew up with.

Being presented with a situation that has no societal or experiential script is a challenge. And not one I was up to for several years. All that could be done was to hang on to the coat tails of convention and put trust in a range of professionals. The immediate issue was to keep as tight as grip as possible on convention; 'fixing' him to deal with the present.

Many people reading this will have come across the uplifting stories of the many autistic people who have been there at the tipping points of history. Less will be aware of the 'Silicon Valley' effect, where highly focused minds have an advantage in terms of information technology development – generating kudos, high incomes, marriages and the pitter-patter of little feet ...and future IT specialists.

Mathematically able autistic people tend to gravitate towards careers in engineering and computing. Their capacity for focused thought can take them to the edge and beyond the boundaries of existing knowledge in their field. There is some evidence that the high salaries associated with their intellectual capital is enabling these people to attract mates. Consequently, in the silicon valleys of the industrialised world more autistic people are getting married and having children. Autistic neurology is probably a genetically disseminated condition, ergo – more autistic people.

This is a group of autistic people who *have* benefited *materially* from mainstream education.
Such opportunities should never be denied – just made easier and less risk ridden.

For the 90% of people who don't end up in aspie valley – work is less easy to come by and keep.

An advert on Radio Kerry was seeking somebody to work part-time in a sports shop. The applicants had to …

- **be good team players**
- **be able to take the initiative**
- **have good communication skills**
- **have good organisational skills**

I'm sure they weren't deliberately trying to exclude people with AS – but their requirements come across as a check-list of relative weaknesses in the profile of a typical 'aspie'.

A lack of interview stage skills is of course another huge issue

Neither should we forget that bullying doesn't stop when the school uniform gets ditched. It is rife in some organisations. All the traits that made our lads targets at school will attract the predators once again.

An unconventional route to work may prove a better option.

It wasn't too long ago that Sean came in the door from his first hour of paid employment. He was paid 5 euro for odd-jobbing at the local organic market. It was a milestone that gave his self-esteem a huge boost. We have engineered a series of structured challenges that he has taken on and succeeded in. This rising confidence added to his innate decency and honesty will stand him in good stead. His opportunities may well develop *organically* in more than one sense.

This bears comparison with the conventional route into paid employment.

My son needs to be in an environment with a bit of slack in it. This has to be engineered. His self-esteem is incompatible with a pressurised post where people might see his difficulties as an opportunity to poke fun or bully or be exasperated.

Voluntary work may be the answer for some; there is no pecuniary pressure and more leeway for relaxed interaction.

There is a local supported employment scheme for people with disabilities. It seems likely we will be heading down that route when he is 18.

There is some evidence that people with Asperger Syndrome can do well in such schemes.

In a study conducted by Lynn Mawhood and Patricia Howlin, St Georges Hospital Medical School,

'Positive outcomes were noted for adults who had systematic support to get and keep work over a 2 year period. Compared to a control group without support, the thirty supported individuals, on average, ended up in better jobs with better pay and fewer periods out of work.

They highlight, in particular, the cost-effectiveness of close liaison with employers in order to match vacancies to the interests and aptitudes of the job seekers. I believe this reinforces the value of identifying 'vocationally exploitable' interests early, and nurturing them.

Even at the expense of 'jack of all trades' academic education.

Being in and out of work can be worse than being out of work.

Unless a person belongs to the academic elite of the Asperger Syndrome community, joining the work-force *without* support is probably a bad idea. It is more likely to result in a chequered employment record and this is not good for the maintenance of mental health. The periodic stress and strain of 'job – unemployment – job – unemployment ' is **not** a scenario you would wish for anybody. But it is especially vital for somebody with Aspergers Syndrome to avoid it.

"Loss of confidence is also a factor. If you haven't worked for a long time or are getting turned down regular or have tried loads of jobs and they have never worked out, then of course psychologically it is going to affect you...... in any of these disastrous scenarios s/he will lose the relative security that the previous Benefits had offered.... somebody could receive no money whatsoever for 26 weeks. How are people with this condition ever going to get jobs representing their true level when they are living in fear of losing their benefits. Much has to be considered before someone with AS is forced into employment and it is vital that the people who make these decisions are made aware of the implications...."

Kevin Phillips (website)

Creating a world of uncertainty and fear is a sure fire way of calling up mental health issues in autistic people. It just doesn't make sense to create this type of employment pattern. And it can be avoided – at least to a large extent – by supported employment programmes.

A degree from the University of Life may be better .

Having a degree is no guarantee of securing a graduate job. The Higher Education Statistics Agency reports that 38% of graduates are stacking shelves and answering phones six months after finishing their course. (Matthew Taylor, Guardian 3/1/05) And if your social and interview skills are diminished by AS, the likelihood of paying off all those student debts any time soon is correspondingly diminished. New under-graduates in England can expect to finish their studies with an average £15,000 debt around their neck.

Graduates of Engineering and Computing – favourites for the numerically adept sub-section of autistic people – may fare better than this but they still have to attend interviews. The point being that once again the apparent benefits of a conventional path to 'success' are called into question when we look just beyond the hype and the spin. The benefits of pushing people through academic courses must be viewed warts and all. There is a downside. The average starting salary for a graduate in the UK is only £17,000.

And University *can* be a miserable place for those who find it difficult to mix. Neither is it devoid of predators and piss-takers.

The traditional extra-curricular pursuits that make University *fun* are also less accessible to an autistic person. Given there is an understandable pride in having one's offspring graduate, once again we need to be aware of our ego in the decision making process. This much trumpeted route may once again be wasting time that could be spent on establishing a sustainable life-style.

It comes down to a series of trade-offs

I am not an academic in the field of autism . But as far as I can make out, the part of the spectrum that an autistic person is deemed to inhabit *seems* to be determined by the level of their IQ. Commentators do speak of different levels of 'IQ' at different segments of the spectrum.

Many children are seen to move along the spectrum as they mature.
This would generally be identified by adults as a good thing i.e. progress.
So it's understandable that we try to help children with this movement along the spectrum.

But why is just *one* type of intelligence used to define
'progress'? We know other kinds of intelligence matters as well.
Indeed social acumen and the state of their 'mental health are factors that will determine the quality of life of our children - as much if not more than their core IQ.

Yet the conventional linear spectrum does not seem to encompass such attributes.

Furthermore, 'IQ' per se gets put on the back-burner once they hit the school system: Success in tests and exams is used as a proxy for IQ.
Whether you are level 3 in English and level 5 in geography is what is deemed to matter (England).

But would we really prefer to have a 21 year old with a high 'IQ' i.e. a boxful of exam certs. but unable to articulate their problems to a hospital doctor.

Would we swop academic qualifications for mental health for ourselves?

It might help in thinking about the 'big picture' to expand the spectrum from a linear thing into a 3-dimensional thing incorporating social acumen and mental health.

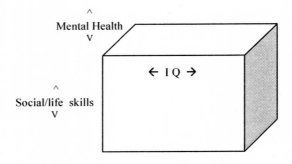

With the variables being -
    (a) IQ (or proxy)
    (b) social/life competence
    (b) mental health.

There can be significant trade-offs between these variables e.g. being rushed and harried along the 'academic' axis may result in regression on the mental health axis.

This will blow back as regression on the academic axis once a tipping point is reached.

If chronic stress induces depression this will cause regression in all 3 facets.

Also, exclusive focus on 'academic' material will result in inertia on the 'social/life competence' line; as there is no time for coping skills to be taught.

We need to switch the risks from children to those with a legal responsibility to provide an appropriate education.

In Greenfield, Wisconsin a teenager is in the process of suing his school for setting too much holiday homework thus allegedly ruining his Summer holidays. This is cited as an example of 'compensation culture' gone mad. I'm not so sure. The young man had secured a job as a 40-hour a week summer camp counsellor. Surely he must have learnt so much in this laudable pursuit. And had a reasonable claim for time to 'chill out ' in the evenings.... rather than struggle with calculus.

Children in these islands are lambasted for irregular attendance at school. Rarely is the relevance of the diet they are fed at school the subject of attack. Voting with your feet is particularly understandable if you are struggling academically **and** being bullied. It is an increasing source of consternation to me that we get away with putting children in harm's way for no good reason. Many of our 'trouble-makers' hold down part-time jobs where they are respected and valued. In less exam-oriented times they would be embarking on apprenticeships of a formal or non-formal nature.

Of course, the risks are particularly acute for autistic children in mainstream schools. The incidence of depression and suicide is testimony to the risks that are taken with such children. The anecdotal evidence from those who have been through the experience is overwhelming and damning. In fact the evidence is such that nobody can claim to be ignorant of the risks being taken with autistic adolescents.

Consequently we are now in a position to switch the risks from the child to the education provider. If the bureaucrats and the politicians were wary of legal action being taken due to psychological injuries they would be a lot less glib about '*including*' autistic people in hugely stressful environments.
Or of dragging their feet when extra supportive resources are sought.

To be fair there are very few decision makers who would *knowingly* put vulnerable children in life-threatening situations. But that's just it –like most teachers and doctors they are busy and they don't know much about autism. Their wake-up call is less likely to come from parents than solicitors. Horrible. But that's the way things get prioritised. And our children's health is too precious to pussyfoot about with. They have a system and a budget to protect. We have a child to protect. They have no brief for our child's mental health. We have to factor it in to their thinking.

Not all Politicians are… politicians.

In contrast to the succession of here-today-gone-tomorrow Education Secretaries who have turned English secondary schools in fear-driven exam factories, there *are* a few Politicians who actually champion the cause of our 'non-standard inputs'. Foremost amongst these - and given my political leanings I never thought I'd say this - is Conservative MP, Angela Browning. She has periodically educated the House of Commons on Asperger Syndrome. On 23/10/01 she said,

"Initially [AS] may sound rather quirky, but not like a major disability. …many adults with AS may be well educated' but are unable to manage cooking or

even seek appropriate help if they have a physical medical condition. Many suffer bullying at school which affects their self-esteem and often stays with them for the rest of their lives. Inappropriate behaviour, which is often a normal autistic response, is frequently seen by other adults as intimidating. At worst, mental health professionals misdiagnose it. It is not uncommon for adults with AS to be sectioned under the Mental Health Act or prescribed drugs, because their autistic behaviour.. is misdiagnosed as a mental health problem. That is not to disregard the fact that mental health problems occur, and one does not have to be a psychiatrist to understand why. Factors include growing into adulthood with no friends, having no social life...never forming personal relationships that lead to marriage, poor job opportunities, denied the opportunity to drive a car.... it is no wonder that depression is common, that mental health problems develop on top of autism and that the suicide rate is high. It costs tens of thousands of pounds a year to support somebody who presents in crisis.... input is needed before the crisis occurs. 46% of people did not receive a diagnosis until after the age of 16. Sufferers carry no white stick, and on a good day, one would wonder whether they had a problem at all. Those who suffer from AS are discriminated against because they have a life-long disability but are also intelligent. Since when has IQ prevented the recognition of a disability? AS is a form of autism characterised by abnormalities of reciprocal interaction. One of our top priorities must be to raise the awareness of the syndrome in primary care and in all services. On 10/9/03 she elaborated further on the issues facing people with AS and their families. AS is not an illness. Management of the condition is best addressed by individually tailored packages of support. They will not cure the condition – it is lifelong- but they will vastly improve the quality of life for the sufferer and maximise their opportunities for living independently. Behaviour may be challenging.... almost always triggered by events rather than an emotional response. Very few provincial psychiatrists have been trained in either the diagnosis or management of AS and even fewer [can] differentiate between a mental health condition and what [is] normal autistic behaviour.... day after day people with AS are admitted to mental health hospitals.... it is all too common for psychiatrists even to ignore an existing diagnosis of AS....

they are often treated with strong drugs that have little or no effect on the symptoms...why should it address the symptoms if the underlying cause is physiological.

Brilliant stuff, Mrs Browning

In Ireland we are lucky to have Kathy Sinnot MEP .The mother of an autistic child she famously fought the state on behalf of her child. I was very happy to share the platform with her at an aspire Conference in Cork recently. She was as insightful as Mrs Browning.

Lighting the candle

The two most useful things I've read about AS have a common theme i.e. respect for the individual who actually has it.

Talking of life with his autistic son, Nobel prize winner Kenzaburo Oe reflected,

"I feel human beings can heal themselves; the will to be healed, and the power of recovery are very strong in us. That's the most important thing I've learnt in my life with my son.

And then there's Rebecca Moyes – a teacher and the parent of an autistic child,

"Providing our children with the gift of self-esteem is always more effective than every dollar we spend on therapy and treatment to 'fix' Asperger Syndrome. "

The parents of every newly AS diagnosed child should be given a credit card size copy of these beautiful statements – one on each side -to keep about their person.

If we treat their difficulties as delays rather than deficits.
If we respect their passions.
If we define success in an appropriate way.
If we do these things - we are not being naïve;
we are just boxing very very clever.

It isn't easy parenting an adolescent with Asperger's Syndrome but....

You will not be lied to - and if you are you will greet it as progress

You will become an expert on several topics you previously knew little about

You will not be pestered for the latest trainers - and if you are you will greet it as progress

You will not have to put up with teenage sleep-overs.

You will not be punched by the father of the girl your son made pregnant

You will not find recreational drugs in his pockets

You will be your child's best friend at a time when other parents are being side-lined in favour of peers..

You will know *exactly* what to buy for birthdays and Christmas

You will not have arguments with him about whether he comes on holiday with you

You will have loads of respite time - as long as you leave him to his 'passion'

Music Therapy

My son takes himself off to listen to music and dance several times a day. Wikipedia describes music therapy as,

.. the use of <u>music</u> by a trained professional to achieve <u>therapeutic</u> goals. Goal areas may include, but are not limited to, motor skills, social/interpersonal development, cognitive development, self-awareness, and spiritual enhancement.

But there is no trained professional involved in Sean's therapy – just the person who has most to gain from the self-therapy. It's not something I initiated either .

He loves the Beatles and Elvis - and will trawl through charity shop collections for rare and collectible versions of their work .

It is too easy to underestimate the role of the person who has the most to gain from the acquisition of new skills; and think the power to 'fix' things lies in our hands only. We need to give them time and space to put their own antidotes in place. And sensitively nurture and respect these antidotes. Music and dance takes precedence over anything else in our curriculum. Because it's his module; it's what he feels he needs to do. And it does him good. .

When the student is ready the teacher will appear?

All children - especially autistic children – do learn best via a curriculum that is *personalised* not pre-determined by politicians and academics for delivery by a subject teacher in a certain term in a certain year.

In a conventional school setting – getting up and saying
' Bye – I'm off to listen to Elvis for a bit' wouldn't go down too well.
Well, not if teacher couldn't go too!

An early diagnosis should be less difficult now

The monotopical monotone monologues; the inability to interact with peers; the atypical level of distress brought on by loud noises; the 'little professor' phrases; the lack of eye contact; the flapping hands; the repetitive and ritualistic actions; the obsession with a particular topic.

I think you would be 'unlucky' to present a verbal six year old displaying these traits to a Consultant today and not come away with a diagnosis of High Functioning Autism / Aspergers Syndrome. If this is not the case then negligence has supplanted ignorance as the key factor.
And whilst anecdotal evidence from parents does tend to indicate on-going frustrations with diagnosis, the numbers being diagnosed has gone up.
Some of the less enlightened media talk of an *autistic epidemic* as if it were an illness like measles. The increase in numbers means either the diagnostic tools are trawling in people who would previously have been missed. Or there is an 'environmental' factor at work producing a higher incidence of autism than previously was the case: In this respect there are many potential 'culprits' but the jury is out on all of them.

It seems to be generally accepted that the biggest factor is the improvement in diagnostic tools and techniques.

Tony Attwood's excellent book '**Asperger's Syndrome – A guide for parents and professionals**' provides a good resume of the screening and diagnostic tools that exist. Some of these are for parents and health visitors to employ. They are being refined all the time.
The big question now is how widely they are disseminated and used.

There is the **CHAT (Childhood Autism Test)** This enables health visitors to screen for autism even as early as the 18 month 'MOT'. It consists of questions to the parent such as 'does your child ever use their index finger to point out things or ask for things'. The questions are supplemented by observation of the child's reaction to certain tasks e.g. having got the child's attention, how does the child respond when you point at an object and say 'oh, look, there's a.' Is the child's attention drawn to the object. Do they look across to see what you are pointing at or are they looking at your hand or elsewhere.

There is evidence coming through now that many of these tests are very reliable. If autism is diagnosed early on it is rarely a diagnosis which does not stand the test of time.

In the course of a thirty year career a primary school teacher will get to know nearly a thousand children very well. A secondary school teacher will get to know eight times as many less well. But no child should get to the age of 8 without one of their primary school teachers spotting the tell tail traits.

A misdiagnosis lasting 9 years made life trickier than need be for my son and me. But our experience pales beside some. Sometimes a child with AS responding to environmental stressors will behave in a manner that might be misconstrued as mental illness. Inappropriate volume and echolalia are also common traits in schizophrenia .If a child gets wrongly diagnosed as mentally ill their whole life can be blighted by inappropriate medication and/or incarceration in psychiatric units or prison. It used to happen a lot. It still happens too often.

Teachers who have a working knowledge of autism are in a position to save a life.

We practised drop-kicks from an early age. It felt like the right thing to do.

It was obvious from the outset that he wouldn't be a centre-forward or a nippy winger. He was an ungainly runner with legs and arms not obeying the usual rules. He was *eccentric* in other ways too - so the message was clear.
He could be a goal-keeper!

A game of footy has significance for bonding and integration with male peers. If you are going to get stuck in nets you might as well specialise early. So we practised catching and toe-punts and drop kicks.

I hadn't a clue in the early days about the whole range of sensory and motor delays that were also in play. Up to 90 % of people with Aspergers Syndrome have difficulties with motor co-ordination.

There is then a big overlap with Dyspraxia in this respect, (and in perception and language development).

The inability to join in ball games is one of the things that automatically excludes a child at school.

That's once you've got yourself changed – which tests sequencing skills to the limit. No apparent awareness of dress sense is another issue – and one that becomes more and more important as they get older.

Having the slightest interest in winning is rare amongst 'aspies'.

If a teacher takes charge and 'places' a child with AS in a team, or pairs them up, it breeds resentment from peers who are, unlike our child, naturally competitive.

Eventually the child will want to withdraw from this source of failure and criticism. There are ways of alleviating this.

My son went to a secondary school which catered for people with physical disabilities. Some of the staff ran a Boccia team and he proved to be more than competent at it. His success was acclaimed in the presentation of trophies at year assemblies. This involved putting his disability in the public domain. Nevertheless these were gestures well meant and things like this tinged his departure with sadness.

I am also aware of less enlightened schools where PE teachers have not been as 'imaginative' with children displaying sporting ineptitude. "Hoi… Spaceman" is the starting point for one anecdote when a child was unable to find a gap in the line of other children.

To be fair the teacher concerned was ignorant of the issues that the child was dealing with. As were the child's parents. Even so it wouldn't go down in any teaching manual. Not to say I haven't had my fair share of whispered expletive moments.

Notwithstanding all of this - it is important to keep the physical exercise going and not to let negative experiences hold sway: Endorphins provide a great natural antidote to feeling down and physical activity promotes much needed sensory integration.

A mini-trampoline is a permanent fixture in the middle of our kitchen/garden. When Sean was younger we spent a lot of time in the sand dunes; these are great for the sensory integration exercise of crawling - using arms and legs in tandem to get to the top.
We team up with his cousins to play basketball.
When focused he has an uncanny way of scoring without touching the rim of the basket. It happens too often to be sheer coincidence. In the last year he has become confident enough to tackle and pass the ball.

There is evidence that the root cause of the motor skill problems lies in a part of the brain called the cerebellum. The cerebellum controls such things as muscle tone, balance, posture, and limb movements. In other words the problem is physiological. Getting an occupational therapist involved early can allow great strides to be made – literally.

At a fine (as opposed to gross) motor skill level there are often difficulties with holding a pencil/pen, using it to write legibly and draw. As the core activity at school this will produce no end of frustration and exasperation for all concerned.

Using a knife and fork in a co-ordinated fashion is also difficult. Sometimes chewing and even swallowing is impaired.

Along with kicking a ball, riding a bike presents one of the most important opportunities for social interaction and fun. But it's a lot less socially acceptable if you are nine and the stabilisers are still on.

I spent days trying to 'fix' my son in this respect.

Far from watchful eyes of course.

Then I gave up.

One day when he was 10 he shouted me to come outside. And there he was – riding his bike.

Who was teaching who what?

Desensitisation is best pursued when you know there are sensitivities!

The first ride on a Ghost Train is a rite of passage that most of us have to endure. It only lasts for a few minutes and some of us eventually get to like it. Especially when courting rituals begin. I could not understand his almost super-human strength at resisting my efforts to get him on. He had done it once before. Fair enough - he had screamed most of the way through but that was par for the course first time around. He should have learnt it wasn't fatal by now shouldn't he!

What he had actually experienced was beyond my ken at the time.

Many people with autism are hypersensitive to noise and touch and lights. Add the deliberate unpredictability of the ride to the mixture and you have something close to a real torture chamber for an autistic child.

This sensitivity also explains why taking him to Windsor Castle via Hayes station was fraught with tension - as the Inter-City to Cardiff screamed past the narrow platforms.

And why he dug his nails into my back when the big HOOTER went in the swimming pool at Butlins.

Until we got our sheep-dog pup recently, he still has the stereotypical (for AS people) reaction to dogs. Far too noisy, unpredictable and biological.

Other people with autism report on the difficulty they have with screening out background noises when they need to. This must play havoc with concentration in all but the most repressed classroom.

Sean's sensitivity to sounds seems to have diminished over time.
Some smells also used to produce an over the top response.
Possibly sensitivity to touch explains his aversion to sitting on knees when he was a toddler. All that information flooding in unfiltered must be totally overwhelming. Shutting down seems like a logical response.
So does fixing your attention on **one** familiar thing
– using it as an anchor to combat the tide of sensory information that is sluicing around.

We can reframe most things to help us deal with them

A passion conveys a completely different message to an obsession. Passions are good things you choose to do. Obsessions are bad things you feel driven to do. We can't respect a passion if we misinterpret it as an obsession (and vice-versa)

'Star Trek' is the latest of a series of passions for him, and thankfully, the most age-appropriate and socially acceptable.

The first passion was 'Thomas'.

What is it with **Thomas the Tank Engine**?

Lots of children love Thomas, but not as deeply or for as long as autistic children. If you ever watch a television documentary on autism chances are the music in the background will be from a Thomas video.

Why do these passions play such a big part in their lives? It may be, as mentioned above, that the topic represents a kind of comfort blanket in this confusing world of sights and sounds and people. Here is one small part of a crazy world that has been tamed; that they have made their own and are calling the shots in. It's a bolthole which allows stress levels to subside; an internal flood barrier that can be raised when life gets a bit much. It is, therefore, wise to be very cautious in closing off this escape route.

Thomas, for example, is a therapeutic young tank-engine in several other ways: He allows children to see that actions have a consequence; and distinguish good deeds from bad; to appreciate social interaction around a set of rules which are enforced but frequently broken; he enables children to appreciate that all the other 'people' have minds and viewpoints and friction results from ignoring their needs; he shows what happens when 'people' go too fast; and he helps with impaired visual tracking skills . What a good little engine he is.

My son has an encyclopaedic knowledge of Coronation Street 1960-2006. He has videos and books - we even built our own set once.

And wrote stories.

I am convinced he has taught himself the nuances of social interaction by watching Jack and Vera, Mike and Ken!

He consequently has an appreciation of colloquialisms that - given it's a dying art - is now way beyond the average for any adolescent.

And they have dealt with so many useful topics over the years that he has bent my ear over. There should be a degree in Corrie Studies. He could teach it.

(Interestingly, he is less dogmatic recently about watching *every* episode of the Street. If he has the opportunity to be in company that will take precedence. I interpret this increased flexibility as progress.)

Playstation Therapy.

I've been told of a Headteacher of a special school in England who has secured his 15 minutes of fame by confiscating Playstations from errant students. His complaint was that children who had been diagnosed as 'autistic' were actually just sleepy; staying up late playing games! I'm not sure of the veracity of the tale; I know many teenage boys go through an 'autistic phase but...! This antipathy towards games consuls doesn't tie in with my own experience.

Computer games are far from being a *waste of time* for autistic children.

They allow safe brain workouts to take place.

If you *don't* initiate and plan and adapt your strategy on the Playstation you don't get very far.

The ability to extrapolate is crucial in order for us to operate with speed and confidence in novel situations.

It teaches the value of perseverance and problem-solving too. And is a real social glue for encounters with peers.

He has learnt how to negotiate when trading the games in.

Numeracy and literacy get a boost too.

135

His immature visual tracking skills get a tremendous workout.

And crucially; in our intensive relationship it delivers important 'time-outs' for both of us.

He has probably learnt more skills from playing computer games with his cousins than he has from me.

I think the Headteacher in England is missing an opportunity to exploit a passion. I could build an entire curriculum around Sean's playstation. As in Judo, it's a case of using your opponents energy to your own advantage Angry young people don't make good students.

Star Trek is the best source of cognitive behaviour therapy in the known universe.

In arriving at an interest in Star Trek, my son is following a well trodden path for neurologically different people. Maybe it's because it is awash with characters who need to have human interaction explained to them. Spock, Data, Tuvok, 7 of 9 - all of them require step by step explanations of the nuances of neuro-typical emotions and communication.

He would love access to a holo-deck where he, like the autistic Mr Barclay, would be the life and soul of the party, where all the others hang on his every word, laugh at his jokes, and females swoon at his social aplomb.

We have just watched an episode of Voyager together. 7 of 9 was being admonished for punching an annoying guest on the nose. Captain Janeway tells 7 of 9 that *she* felt like doing it too! But people have to learn the difference between having an impulse and acting upon it.

Another very useful point of tangency with young people is his love of the Simpsons – where again he has an almost encyclopaedic knowledge.

Home education is a valid and legal alternative to 'school'.

There is a good deal of legal support for alternative provision if you feel your child's mental health is best served outside the mainstream. Article 29 of the UN Convention on the rights of the child says,

Parties agree that the education of the child shall be directed to: The development of the child's personality, talents and mental and physical abilities to their fullest potential.

Only two eligible countries in the world have not yet signed up to the Convention: Somalia and the USA. This makes it the most popular human rights treaty in the world.

The European Convention on Human Rights (ECHR) as interpreted by the European Commission and Court of Human Rights is also pertinent. Article 2 of the First Protocol to the Convention provides:

No person shall be denied the right to education. In the exercise of any functions, which it assumes in relation to education and to teaching, the State shall respect the right of parents to ensure such education and teaching in conformity with their own religious and philosophical convictions.

If your 'philosophy of education' involves a more holistic approach, fostering personal development, independent living and the preservation of mental health, article 2 is a useful law with which to pursue flexibility. Merely preparing children to take tests and exams does not constitute an education. Even more so when the child has a glaring need for social and life skills.

In Ireland, article 42 of the constitution states that

'the primary and natural educator of the child is the family'.

It goes on to say that

'Parents shall be free to provide this education in their own homes ...the state shall not oblige parents in violation of their conscience and lawful preference to send children to schools established by the state.'

We are conditioned to think about schooling and education as one and the same thing.

I watched a harrowing documentary last night about an Irish teenager with autism. His loving parents were doing their best to find a placement for him – it wasn't proving easy because of his autistic traits and behaviour patterns. The state was culpable in their lack of empathy towards a very troubled young man. The pop-up information box outlining the content of the programme was dispassionate: Despite all the mayhem and tears it described the content as being about a boy who *hadn't been to school for two years.*

The notion of 'school' is one of society's lynchpins; it is at the very core of what right thinking people think should be happening between the ages of 4-18. Fair enough. But this makes **not** being at school seem ...wrong.

Talking about truancy last week an MP said with confidence
' If you don't go to school you don't get an education.'
Some elective home-educators would quibble with this.

Tony Attwood has been a crucial source of insight into AS for me.

His books and lectures have helped me to put my son's difficulties into a context. I attended his conference in Cork two years ago. Brilliant man. This is his take on home education for children with Aspergers Syndrome.

"There has been some success in reducing anxiety and increasing scholastic attainment by scheduled breaks during the term, part-time enrolment or home tuition. Parents and teachers may be aware that the term has been too long for the child and they are showing signs of chronic anxiety. As much as a child who is physically ill may have a few days off school, the child with AS may need a few days off to relax, enabling them to cope till the end of the term. Some children are enrolled only for morning classes and return home in the afternoon. School work is undertaken during the afternoon but alone and supervised by a parent. When anxiety is extreme full time home tuition has proved successful, especially with teenagers....... this approach can be a constructive alternative to strong medication and possible admission to a psychiatric unit."

I love the understatement in that last sentence!!!

As mentioned above, I am not an elective home-educator.

Given our unique circumstances, it was simply the best solution to the problem we were faced with.

In a system that was *really* trying to include autistic children we would have **Life Coaches** appointed to guide the children through their adolescent years. And these versatile people would have teacher status pay and clout. If the Sheffield statistics (see later) are typical there is £30,000 per child 'in the kitty'.

An **AS Life Coach** might have a caseload of 2 autistic children.

In a school of 1000 children there might be 4 children with diagnosed Aspergers Syndrome (conservative estimate) ; resulting in 2 life coaches who could support each other's work. They would have responsibility for liaison with the Primary school so that all that corporate knowledge about the child is not lost in the move to big school. They would be trained up in Cognitive Behaviour Therapy and Solution Focused Brief Therapy. They would be the daily link between home and school. They would be responsible for the child's work-life balance; be sensitive to mood and disposition; be the moderator for when to push on and when to retreat; be the fielder of bullying issues; and the teacher of the million and one skills that other children pick up via the 'hidden curriculum'. They would be the person that ensures the child gets individualised physical activity every day.

Unlike most mainstream 'inclusion units' the criteria for success for the Life Coach would **not** be the % of 'normal' lessons attended: The focus would be the delivery of a pre-determined and individualised programme, using the resources of the institution flexibly.

We have to ditch the notion that their salvation lies in helping them back to the *normality* of 10 GCSE / Junior Cert. courses. We need to teach them enterprise skills and set up mini-businesses based on their passions. Until education authorities provide Life Coaches for children with AS then the job has to be taken on by parents – or it won't get done. We should send them the bill.

Solution – Focused Brief Therapy is a good tool to have in the toolbox.

People with Depression usually get a few minutes with the doctor and a prescription for anti-depressants. This isn't good; the fifth biggest killer in the USA is the abuse and aside effects of legally prescribed drugs. In the light of recent research highlighting the enhanced risk of suicide, the NHS has now told doctors to stop giving anti-depressants to people under the age of 18. It suggests that children with mild depression should be given advice on diet and exercise. In more serious cases non-drug therapy should be employed. This may be easier said than done; less than half the people in England with mental health problems currently get access to a 'talking therapy'. Therapists trained in Cognitive Behaviour Therapy (CBT) or Solution-Focused Brief Therapy (SFBT) etc, are in short supply.

SFBT is a no-nonsense 'listening and acting' therapy. I trained in this therapy with Eileen **Murphy Consultants.** I liked it so much I joined the company:

www.brief-therapy-uk.com. The principles and techniques of SFBT were developed in the 1950's by Milton Erickson to help people with severe and chronic mental health problems. Solution Focused Brief Therapy (SFBT) has a respect for the client's strengths at its core. Nobody can benefit from interventions which focus exclusively on failings. Instead, we need to start with the premise that our child has huge potential which might be realised through nurturing their attributes.

As Kevin Satchwell, Headteacher of Thomas Telford School put it for children in general,

" ...finding that one small thing that makes children feel good about themselves... and nurturing it."

Philosophically there would be a good deal of overlap between SFBT and the Son Rise Programme or Floor time. SFBT tries to draw out existing strengths, competencies, and strategies to move the client away from the problem and towards a sustainable personalised solution.
SFBT is pragmatic not dogmatic.
It recognises that both the individual and the problem are unique and therefore the solution will be also be unique.

One of the most useful techniques used by SFB therapists is the isolation of the *Achilles heel* of the 'problem' by identifying 'exceptions' For somebody suffering from depression, the identification of times when it the depression is less debilitating can be the signpost for an effective intervention. For people with AS there is often an area of extreme interest, even expertise. Tapping into, respecting, and nurturing this passion can deliver a point of tangency with the 'neuro-typical' world, interaction with others, self-esteem, and possibly a vocational path.

Huge amounts of resources are invested in trying to 'fix' weaknesses in our children – even though many of the 'weaknesses' only exist relative to transitory institutional expectations.

SFBT has a baseline of where a person actually *is*, not where we would like them to be.

If this involves operating 'outside the box' so be it: Milton Erickson had a patient who thought he was Jesus. Nothing and nobody was shifting that notion. Erickson got him work doing carpentry around the hospital!

In football parlance this is called 'playing the way you are facing'. It is a very empowering mindset because it invites you to use the resources you and your child already have, rather than just running after health and education bodies in an often futile attempt to get them to *fix your* child.

Problem solving skills do not come as standard in the autistic portfolio. So passing on a 'can solve' mentality is hard but crucial work – if living independently is the objective.

Somehow, the willingness to take the initiative to seek out solutions has to be hard-wired in them while we have the chance. .

The first step in this direction is adopting a solution-focused mindset ourselves.

This involves embracing the inescapable fact that they have a neurological difference. And then getting on with helping them to diminish the impact it has on their lives.

And to tell them what we are doing and why we are doing it – being open and honest about their 'delays'.

As then, as soon as they are old enough, collaborating with them on the choices that exist.

Next, with fingers and toes crossed, let them make the choices. And talk through the good ones and get the ones that don't work out into perspective.

In essence it is no different to the route taken by all parents and children. In some ways it is no more difficult either.

That *change is inevitable*, is another key message from the Solution Focused approach.

I have to stop myself being over-protective of him. I know it was right to put distance between us and a regime of chronic stress. But it *is* possible to go too far in the opposite direction too. I have to expose him to as many novel and difficult situations as possible. If I don't then I do him a big disservice: All I would be doing is postponing the 'meltdown' until I am not around to manage the situation.

Personal Navigation needs to kick in.

Change was evident when creepy creatures first emerged from the slime half a billion years ago. The first thing they did was eat each other. The ones that are still around today are the ones that could best adapt to change.
As Darwin observed,

"It is not the strongest of the species that survive, nor the most intelligent, but the ones most responsive to change." –Charles Darwin

Given that our children are often *averse* to change, one of the most important things we can do is cajole them into new experiences where they face carefully chosen challenges that move them on from their current level of expertise.

Mainstream school can indeed *challenge* the individual – but in a massive overwhelming way rather than a managed therapeutic way.

Growing your own school is another option

In Hillingdon, West London, a couple of parents have done just that. Unhappy with the choices on offer for their autistic children, Anna and Sean Kennedy re-mortgaged their house to set up their own school. I know the building they have taken over well - we used to have NASUWT meetings there. The funding for places will come from the local authority. The determination and courage needed to take on the system in this way is exceptional.

We can teach *skills* in a formal way.

The use of 'Social Stories' seems to be increasingly well established for the transmission of appropriate 'rules of engagement' for different social settings. For more details it would be worth finding about the structure suggested by Carol Grey – a leading light in this area. I have no evidence as to the efficacy of her approach but a lot of people seem to think they are very good.

It should be possible to devise your own exercises to address all the other 'coping skills' too, including 'mental health skills'.
My sessions with my son have developed in an ad hoc fashion.
I could have been more systematic.

In the case of helpful mental health 'skills / attitudes' it is possible to take each desirable attribute and deliver 'lessons' to elicit that attribute.

For example, if, for example, we want our children to be able to

' take disappointments in their stride'

we might draw on their frustrations with 'level' games on the computer/games station. (another use!)

Most will have experienced this and yet decided against ejecting said Playstation out the window.

It's a good basis for a role-play and a discussion.

If I were dealing with this issue with my son I might also ask him to think about a long serving character in Coronation St, and ask him to make a list of adverse incidents that have happened to them.

Because of what is at stake, such lessons have more validity than the academic lessons foregone. And at least equal validity with the ones that remain. *Not* being able to deal with relatively minor setbacks is a huge time-consuming issue for autistic adolescents. To the extent such lessons help to develop a sense of perspective there will be an enormous positive spin-off for everybody at school ...and at home. It just makes no sense to leave issues like this to chance.

The provision of a tri-partite curriculum from the outset is what is required:

The 3 parts being:

Academic study: There has to be a place for the acquisition of the three Rs. This adds to the fact that we need to find some sort of accommodation with a Primary School. The dark arts that lead a child to being able to read and write are known to few. As a secondary school teacher I am in awe of my primary colleagues.

Life/coping skills: The quality of life for our children will depend more on acquiring these skills than on any batch of exam certificates. If not now, then when? If not us, then who? If we crowd these skills out 11-18 the answers are never and nobody. They will not learn them incidentally.

Rest & Recreation: Children with AS get very tired from having to manage the double-whammy of secondary school and adolescence. Plus - they often have huge potential that should not get mulched beneath the exam steamroller; time should be set aside for nurturing their interests.

The precise balance of the curriculum must depend on the individual's initial endowments. We have to give these children a personalised not a nationalised curriculum. Much lauded Individual Education Plans (IEPs) are primarily geared to service the latter – and in my experience rarely get read from one review to the next by busy classroom teachers. (Unless the Inspectorate is coming down the drive.)

Personalised education is a more ambitious construct than an IEP because the 'E' bit is more widely defined in order to create a relevant curriculum. We are stepping outside the box rather than just ticking it! And, for children with AS, it would also address the issues of when, where, and how they can best be taught their curriculum.
Provision might, therefore, be adapted in the following ways:

A reduced academic load - which nevertheless fulfils all minimum matriculation requirements at third level. No doors need be closed by imaginative provision. Very few junior certs/GCSE's are needed to still fulfil matriculation – even at places like Cambridge, TCD et al. Third level institutions *are* aware of AS.

We have more elbow room than we think 11-16

Time to do homework in school. Children with AS are easily fatigued by the demands of the school -day. Their heads need a rest in the evening. Homework can actually be counter-productive. The anxiety it causes can interfere with sleep patterns and leave the child even more vulnerable the next day.

The provision of more one-to-one teaching. If this sounds expensive try adding up all the time used in school to calm down a chronically distraught child.

The provision of tuition in well behaved groups. Children with AS need a learning environment with a minimum of stimuli. Does it really matter if this class is the same age or ability as the child; it's easier for a teacher to help a child with AS if (a) the rest of the group are high-flying /mature/ self-motivated (b) the child is not stressed and distracted by the behaviour of others. It might simply mean the Head of Dept. taking the child into their teaching group.

Twilight or Saturday lessons. Anathema to most, but some teachers *will* volunteer if (a) they know what's at stake (b) the time is included in their teaching load.

Part-time attendance / gap days. These might also be viewed as 'mental health' days/half-days. They represent a solution not a problem.

Strategies to make positive use of unsupervised times such as break and lunch.

Avoidance of corridors between lessons. Transit between some lessons to be tailored to needs. Many children with AS - and some teachers - are terrified of noise and movement on this scale. The trauma stays with the child in the recipient classroom – concentration levels suffer accordingly.

Lessons dedicated to life/coping/personal navigation skills. With support hours being at a premium we need to be focused firmly on the future needs of the child rather than the short-term needs of the institution. Having them do different things from their peers is part of the solution not part of the problem.

Infusion of the general curriculum with material which increases empathy for 'different' children / stand alone items in Personal & Health Ed. Talks to students by students with AS.

Respect for and nurturing of 'passions' e.g. via a mini-enterprise. Imagine if somebody had insisted on Michaelangelo and Einstein following a National Curriculum to the letter!

Awareness raising training for all staff – *focused on the individual* more than the generalities of Aspergers Syndrome.

An individualised physical education programme. Exercise is very important for gross motor skills / sensory integration, yet most children with AS are effectively excluded. If somebody is needed who can supervise them on a trampoline in the morning - whilst the others throw javelins - then the payback will come in the afternoon. Children with AS have huge amounts of stress to 'burn off' and yet they get less opportunities to do so.

The suspension of standard sanctions. Doctors aren't expected to treat people with broken legs the same as people with headaches; if behaviour is **induced** by the hostile environment - and unreasonable demands on atypical neurology - is it fair or professional to punish the behaviour.

Built-in 'Solution-focused' / Cognitive Behaviour'- based counselling sessions. Any sympathetic talking therapy will make a positive difference – and provide respite from the madding crowd. ..... and any number of other adjustments deemed necessary by the parents and the school. There should be no sacred cows – given what's at stake. Some '*subject fundamentalists*' in school will *still* regard this amount of flexibility as an unwarranted nuisance. But many *will* respond positively if they are told what's going on and **why** (a novel idea!).

Personalised Education for children with AS is a win-win-win-win-win initiative.

Teachers win - because the child is being catered for imaginatively and flexibly. S/he isn't just another square peg they are expected to squeeze through a round hole, in an hour, in a hut, with 29 others.

Children win - because the flexible provision brings down their stress levels and makes the onset of Depression less likely. And elbow room is secured for all sorts of things they need to be taught.

Society wins - by having one more included citizen and worker. And the taxpayer gets a huge return on a modest up-front investment.

Parents win - by not having energy, finance and morale sapping fights with the State over interventions that in any case are largely unproven in their efficacy. Their energy thus saved can be focused directly on the child. Schools win by actually being able to offer parents the expertise they crave – instead of just muddling by with (a) good intentions and a fixed smile and/or (b) an annoying 'teacher knows best' attitude.

We should also be flexible about the venue of the learning. For some children - in large conurbations where all options exist - a personalised mix of mainstream, specialist school, and home may be appropriate.

A plateau is safer than a peak.

I listened with interest to Jackie McCormack of Gloucestershire Group Homes when she gave a presentation in Dublin last year.

She cautioned against a mindset that relentlessly pursues 'progress'; pushing people into places they cannot sustain without support levels that may not always be there.

The implication was to find a plateau where somebody is *happy* and then set up base camp for a while.

149

Striving to achieve full *'normality'* is an objective derived from somebody else's value system. I am aware of several people who have reacted badly to continuous pressure to 'improve' especially when that improvement was to be measured purely in terms of paper qualifications.

Should every hard won step towards 'normality' be the catalyst for another and another. I think we need to put progress 'in the bank' and take time to weigh up the costs and the benefits of the next step.

It can be a case of 'Less is more'.

We cannot forever be giving them the impression that they are still not good enough. If attempts to rectify a perceived deficit are proving costly in terms of time and energy - - then leave it alone for a while. In my experience the 'problem' rarely gets fixed while I'm looking at it. And often, with time, even the things that don't get 'fixed' seem less of a big deal. I wish I'd spent less time sweating the small stuff and more time telling him it was all going just fine

The 'Conventional Wisdom' is an oxymoron waiting to happen

I think that the drive to 'educate' most autistic children in large institutions full of noisy unpredictable teenagers might soon be seen as illogical.

The **conventional wisdom** is often an oxymoron waiting to happen.

There was a time when scientists thought the best way to propel rockets into space was via the use of several simultaneously exploded nuclear bombs. There will, I believe, come a time when the quasi-inclusion of autistic children in mainstream secondary schools following a conventional curriculum will seem just as misguided.

'Mainstreaming' autistic children, **without adequate flexibility or support,** will soon be seen in the same light as contracting out cleaning in hospitals or privatising the railways - with the outcome for some individuals being equally disastrous.

The natural response to a stressed-out child in tears is to want to help and protect them. But in protecting them from the hostile environment **we** put them in, we are in danger of fostering dependence rather than independence. The strategies may make perfect sense at the time ,and the children may benefit in the short-term , but what is their **long-term** impact. At some point they will need to be able to navigate their own way through problems. When do we allow them to experience this? Not when we're drilling them for exams, that's for sure. We think we're helping them to survive. We're not – we're doing exactly the opposite.

They need to have an education that involves controlled risk taking – with lots of 'learning at the margin' of their current expertise. It's only *chronic* stress that is to be avoided not engineered and challenging tasks/situations. Employers want flexibility, teamwork skills, and initiative - skills our children are under-endowed with.
How exactly does an over-regimented education rectify this?

Are we not locking in their weaknesses?

Higher education also demands the ability to work independently; constantly doing things *for* the child so they can 'fit in' and 'get on' denies them this skill. Neuro-typical adolescents confront our regimentation as they head for independence– hence the discipline problems we experience!
Even the ones who still co-operate are picking up appropriate post-school skills and attitudes along the way.
But, as we know, children with AS don't learn that much incidentally.
If 'support' consists of helping them to fit in with a regimented and transient institution, then is this really a help or a hindrance?

What happens when the institution bids them farewell?

Anecdotal evidence suggests this is a prime time for additional problems to arise.

Ferrari M & Sternberg R in (1998) Self Awareness: Guildford Press, develop this key concept of **'Personal Navigation' (PN)**

PN involves exactly what it says on the tin.

If an autistic adolescent has the wind taken out of their sails on a daily basis, or is totally directed by others, they will be very slow to take charge of their life; to 'personally navigate' the next section of the journey.

An inability to indulge in 'personal navigation ' constitutes a huge problem as people enter adulthood. So it would appear a good idea to avoid the continuous failure that undermines it. And scale down the regimentation that militates against it.

Structure *is* important for people with AS, but at some point we have to explicitly foster PN skills.

How this might be done is outlined in an excellent article by Richard Howlin: 'AS in the Adolescent Years' in AS **in Adolescence ed Liane Holliday Willey: Jessica Kingsley Publishers.**
Failure to develop this skill results in passivity or inertia –at the opposite end of the spectrum from the independence that we are seeking to promote. An audit of current school experience might flag up few opportunities for developing PN; the *last* thing I wanted in my classroom was 30 *personal navigators* (though judging the number of children who bunk off school, some degree of PN does exist!).

A significant step towards developing PN skills is the affirmation of a person's existing skills and coping strategies. This can involve talking about 'their uniqueness' and their perspective on AS. Then engineering a small 'vacuum' which they can fill with an idea of their own to make life better.

People in general are always best persuaded by solutions they have discovered for themselves. It has to be good for a young person, used to inefficacy, to feel they are *now* instrumental in sorting their life out.
And that they are being listened to.
And *something* is changing for the better because *they* have articulated an idea. All of this takes time.
That time, in my view, is quite legitimately taken from a more traditional curriculum.
The big question is whether an exam-focused institution could ever be farsighted and flexible enough to hand over this time.

St Kevin's should have been Plan A

Each year spent free from chronic stress should be relished in its own right .It doesn't have to be a means to an end. Every day enjoyed at the age of 12 matters mightily for its own sake. And each year spent free of chronic stress is a year spent building up resilience – and ultimately enhances life chances in a way that slavish adherence to a politicised education system cannot.

I have come to believe that what is done is less important than what is **not** done.
A very supportive and ever so slightly cynical friend refers to my house as **St Kevins'.** Sean has attended St Kevins for nearly 4 years now. The nativity play causes a few headaches and the staff Christmas party is a bit dull; no end of night slow dance snog to turn faces red in the new year.
On the other hand Ofsted don't have jurisdiction in this part of the world.
We observe all religious and state holidays.
Sleep and Exercise are lynchpins for the curriculum.
The school Motto is **'Play the way you are facing'.**
The mission statement is **'To chill out and learn a bit '.**

- Kevin Foley -

The big disadvantage of Home Education is the relative poverty that comes with it. I have the Dept. of Education to thank for it not being absolute poverty. Also on the down side, there have been (surprisingly rare) days when one or both of us is sick of the sight of the other of us.

That said there are big advantages too.

No being left in line as the last one to be picked for the football team (yes, it still happens in school).

No ball/social games that can't be fathomed.

No more standing near the perimeter fence while others play around you.

No chasing conversations with peers who don't want to have one.

No bullying

No shouting…. well, not much.

No jostling.

No queues.

No frantic mornings with clothes on back to front

P.E. now consists of unencumbered running down the beach and scrambling up a couple of big dunes. This gets the heart pumping and those endorphins flowing. Sensory integration gets a big boost on those dunes too.

Being able to fly to Rome last March for next to nothing and get off-season priced accommodation; we couldn't afford this when I was working full-time. He did a brilliant project on Rome with materials gathered whilst there. In June two years ago he sat his History Junior Certificate (GCSE) at the secondary school over the road and obtained a grade B. He had no additional time allowance or assistance. It would have been andA' but for the questions involving photo/picture evidence; he finds scanning such material and eliciting information tricky.

He's just done his Leaving Cert. History (A/AS level). The grade is immaterial He's done his best.

The experience will also stand him in good stead should he wish to sit more exam in the future. He's had a controlled dose of the 'feelings' associated with being in an exam room. And he's dealt with them.

We had just returned from a couple of days researching our family history in Dublin. My son having developed an intense interest in Genealogy from his general interest in History and watching the excellent BBC programme,

' Who do you think you are'.

While there we watched a man complaining that the private genealogy service he had already paid was too slow. The germination of a business idea started then. Soon after Sean was regaling all and sundry with his findings at a recent family funeral. And thoroughly enjoying being the centre of attention.

On the back of this he has set up a web-site for the Irish Diaspora to obtain information on who was living in the *auld* family home in 1901 and 1911.

He has had several 'contracts' already but even if it doesn't work out in the long term, he has established a niche in the family – Every generation needs an in-house genealogist – and he has an interesting hobby. The self-esteem derived from having your passion taken seriously and nurtured is massive. It can be an antidote to all the slings and arrows they have to endure. I wish somebody could have told me 17 years ago that things could get as good as this.

Irish Family Tree
Census Search

Sean Foley

Shanahill , Keel
Castlemaine
Co. Kerry

00353877459619

admin@irishroots-census.com
www.irishroots-census.com

Specialist FE provision should be made available to all adolescents with ASDs.

I have tried to include age-specific experiences in our curriculum.

As well as ongoing keyboard skills and 'numeracy for life' sessions which usually involve the local shop, he has had to negotiate more grown up tasks since he turned 16.

He has been on shopping trips involving buses there and back, with a trip to the building society en route to get the cash.

Even scarier – for me- he has planned and executed a journey from Kerry Airport to Stansted – on his own.

Being met on the other side of course.

He has written letters asking for work experience at a local museum.

Also letters to establish his rights re. disability benefits.

His culinary skills are the equal of my own now; most of our meals announce their readiness with a 'ping'

But since he started at the local organic market we are slowly getting 'greener' and healthier.

Socially he has regular interaction with a few of his cousins.

And he has now met up with a lad of about the same age from our local support group – the support group didn't exist until we invented it. Like so many other parents we are carving out provision that doesn't exist.

The Kerry Autism Service has also put together some brilliant sessions on social interaction and anxiety reduction; he has enjoyed making contributions in these sessions and talking to other youngsters with AS.

"Secondary schools and further education are less able to meet the needs of children with autism and Asperger Syndrome and parental satisfaction levels decrease the older their child becomes. Parents struggle to get the provision they believe is right for their child – 64% said that they only achieved satisfactory provision by fighting hard for it. Social skills training is often neglected by schools; greater weight is placed on academic achievement."
Inclusion and Autism: Is it working? by Barnard Prior and Potter NAS.

In Dublin we visited a training centre – 'Tuiscinct' (Understanding). They provide a vocational rehabilitation service for people with AS aged 18 and over. This is an excellent resource. I just think the amount of rehabilitation needed would be less if we had a personalised package from the age of 10.

Relish the milestones that really matter.

When they tell their first white lie to protect somebody else's feeling.
When they tell their first whopper to protect themselves.
When they pick up the phone and arrange something.
When they get a txt from somebody other than a relation.
The solo train trips.
The solo plane trips.
His first dog walk
His first game of darts down the pub
His first genealogy contract
Now these things *really* matter.

(It's the 16th August 2006. It's 10.25. His Leaving Cert History result has just dropped through the door. It doesn't matter what grade he's got. Bloody plastic envelope he's struggling to open. A grade A1. Wow. Self-esteem barometer soaring. More important it was with *his* revision plan. And he stuck to it . It's his result – and he knows it . Wow.)

We should let sleeping teenagers lie

Shakespeare described sleep as "the chief nourisher in life's feast.

New research suggests that the hormonal upheaval of puberty could be the root cause of adolescents loving a lie-in.

One thing is sure - sleep is crucial for teenagers - because it is while they are snoozing that they release a hormone that is essential for growth spurts. They need more sleep than both children and adults.

Many teenagers are sleep deprived.

I know from experience how difficult it can be to teach children who obviously haven't had enough sleep.

Lack of sleep can lead to moodiness, impulsivity and depression. As is often the case with humans we gravitate to self-therapy; so teenagers want to sleep in.

If societal expectations interfere with our physiological needs maybe now and again we should challenge the expectations.

Maybe because we get them up early in the morning they only have enough energy left to grunt at us in the evening.

Is that angst and resentment well deserved; we used to look after their intrinsic needs. Perhaps we get the teenagers we deserve. And god help us when this generation of 'test fodder' gets the reins of power.

They will probably force us to do tests to access state pensions.

In America some schools have delayed the start of their classes to give their teenagers some extra time in bed. One school noticed a significant improvement in the educational performance of its students.

Adolescents with AS operate with levels of stress and anxiety that drains their batteries quickly. School break-times and lunchtimes, which are restorative for neuro-typicals, do not represent a time for winding down for adolescents with AS; exactly the opposite.

So fatigue comes calling and the capacity to learn is further impaired.

I did not have a set time for home school to start.

If he needed a lie-in he got it.

And we didn't start until he had had a shower and done some exercise.

If I had to use a mainstream school for the education of an autistic adolescent I would only send them in the afternoons.

With the mornings being kept for sleeping, stress free reading, surfing the net, watching The Bill and preparing his own school bag for the afternoons.

I would also reclaim evenings from the misery of homework.

Evenings should not elongate the humourless endurance test that exam preparation consists of.

My son was very tired and often overwhelmed by a standard school day.

So the expectation that he work in the evening also was bordering on cruelty Especially since his recording of the work to be done was often less than perfect.

Completing the tasks was often tortuous and time-consuming.

At a time when he should have been watching the Simpsons and having a much needed therapeutic laugh (increasingly seen as vital to health) he was back on a pointless treadmill.

I find it difficult to believe I was party to this conformist regime which now seems to be so obviously not in his best interests.

Incomplete homework was noted by some teachers in his reports.

If only they had been a fly on the wall to see how hard he worked to do what he did.

Evenings also consisted of gradual revelation of the day's frustrations and talking things through so that he could sleep easy and not be anxious about tomorrow. This didn't always work.

Which brings us back to the need for a good nights sleep.

He sleeps very well now and has just hit the 6-foot mark. (4 inches bigger than his dad!)

We need to be wary of agendas that cause chronic interference with sleep, exercise, and laughter.

Laughter is important therapy. We once lost a Batman ball in Tralee Bay. He stood on the shore while I waded deeper and deeper with hands outstretched.

It was always just out of reach and eventually I was up to my chin. He was only young, and for a few minutes it seemed vital that I retrieve *that* ball.

There was some 'fall-out' to deal with when I returned – alive but 'ball-less'! But perhaps not so much as if I had ended up sleeping with the fishes.

We bought another Batman ball. (Solution Focused Mindset).

And the message is?

Chasing the unattainable is plain stupid. .

A daily diet of frustration, exasperation, self-pity, and anger is a recipe for a desperately poor quality of life.

But to the extent we try to adhere rigidly to neuro-typical norms that is exactly what we condemn ourselves and our children to.

 An ongoing series of demoralising experiences.

Where is the joy?

Where is the fun?

Where is the laughter to be both cause and effect of a good life.

If we allow ourselves to be locked into a narrow set of criteria for *success* the feedback is grindingly negative. Well...sod that for a game of soldiers. We need to have a laugh for all sorts of reasons.

And it is a myth that autistic children do *not* have a sense of humour. Many do. It may be a bit dependent on the straightforwardness of the language used but it's often there.

My son loves situation comedies such as Dad's Army and Red Dwarf. If it's a choice between doing homework or laughing at a sit-com it's a moot point as to which is the '*sensible*' option.

The evidence is growing about the efficacy of laughter in reducing the impact of various ailments. Several research teams are now investigating how effective laughter is compared to anti-depressants.

A growing number of hospitals are using clowns as therapy for sick children.

" I see the clowns as healers. When a child begins to laugh, it means he's probably beginning to feel better."
Dr John Driscoll, New York Babies and Children's hospital.

This approach is in marked contrast to our often po-faced interventions that visibly hurt our children's feeling.
How much *fun* is there in extracting geography homework from an already fatigued child.
Nobody else in this world has a holistic brief for our children.
Making sure they have enough rest and fun is a parent's job.

The law of Diminishing Returns applies.

As Tuvok from Star Trek once put it.
"Perfection can sometimes hinder efficiency "
Compromises have to be made. Sometimes the white flag has to fly over the battleground of autistic trait eradication.
 As it should, lest we stray into the business of eradicating a person.
In my experience diminishing returns set in if you try to eradicate a particular trait/deficit completely; every extra hour spent on the issue will deliver less than the previous hour.
The rush of excitement or frustration that floods out of flapping hands and fingers is a case in point. We have an agreement now that this all too visible rush of emotion can be confined to situations where there is no audience.
I have learnt to let all sorts of things go unresolved – ranging from fractions to shoe laces.

In some instances time, maturity and experience(s) plug the gap.
In some instances there are alternative solutions.
In some instances time diminishes the importance of the knowledge/skill; what seemed a big deal is no longer a big deal.

And even if you did manage to stamp on all the foibles, would you finish up with (a) the person you love (b) your sanity. (c) their sanity.

There is nothing in the rulebook that says you have to meet '*failure* head on.
Homer Simpson's philosophy ' if at first you don't succeed …never try again.' has a lot to be said for it.
But time is a great healer.
So are imaginative alternatives until time gets around to it.
Find a way of doing without the skill.
My rule of thumb is to give the priority to things that could (a) cause him emotional pain in the future (b) be deemed as socially unacceptable (c) undermine his chances of living independently.
With time and energy both being limited resources there has to be halfway houses, even with these areas of concern.

Perfection does **not** exist.

Even 'neuro-typicals' get things wrong.

Things *can* work out better for early-school leavers. .

My son is nearly 18 now.
He *is* leggy enough to be a pole-vaulter although he runs with a head nodding style that would put Paula Radcliffe in the h'penny seats.
He is not suffering from depression.
He is positive-minded. The glass is usually half-full .
After so many years of getting things 'wrong', he still needs more re-assurance than the average teenager.
He still employs echolalia to get the task clear in his mind.
He can initiate good conversations, and he goes down the pub on his own to have a soft drink and play darts.

He takes virtually nothing literally now – even the stuff that is meant to be taken literally! Are you being sarcastic, he asks.

He is **very** confident in engaging with other people – as long as they are at least 5 years older; he is still wary of people his own age and younger.

Using the local shop several times a day for the past three years has done his sums a power of good.

He goes into town on the bus on his own; he gets money out of his account and shops and goes for lunch.

His eczema has cleared up.

He will now readily trade an episode of Coronation Street for an unexpected call to socialize - he seems to *need* this bolthole less and less.

He has a grade B junior cert. in History and is awaiting his leaving cert in History result; he did a great project on the reasons why so little census information is available in Ireland. **(Update: He got a grade A1)**

He might give some other subjects a lash in years to come.

He uses the local library for research as well as travelling on his own to the National Archives in Dublin.

He now has an embryonic website (not been on the web-building course yet) which may get him started commercially. If you have Irish roots please go to www.irishroots-census.com. (Did I mention this before?)

He has now graduated from St Kevins.

In the latter stages he operated as a self-directed learner for the most part.

He produced his own revision timetable and stuck to it.

This matters more than any grade he might get.

He has flown to Stansted and back on his own from Kerry Airport.

We had already done the trip a few times and talked and walked it through.

He has a job at the local organic market on a Friday and operates his genealogy stall on a Saturday.

How much of this would be happening if we had persevered with a more conventional path. It's gratifying when people tell us how much progress has been made.

After roughly twenty thousand contact hours, my son would be *very* happy to spend less time with his increasingly grumpy old man.
(And vice versa.)
He can still be exasperating. But thankfully it's more wilful now.
He is better with other people than he is with his old man.
He is significantly less biddable and far more questioning.

Great. Typical bloody teenager!

Repetition of a few key points in case they haven't already been bloody well repeated already.

- If chronic stress can cause mental health problems it is sensible to avoid chronic stress.
- That time is indeed a great healer. We need to give time the time to do its job.
- First – do no harm. Second – don't let anybody else do any harm
- The mainstream education systems in these islands are **not** designed to keep our children mentally healthy. They **are** designed to produce an internationally competitive workforce.
- We shouldn't be relying on the vagaries of school staffing to keep autistic children mentally healthy.
- Teachers are generally not of a mind to *relish* an extra 'challenge' in the classroom i.e. your autistic son or daughter. Castigating them for 'unhelpful' attitudes towards 'inclusion' is pointless They work in a pressurised system that is not of their making. If you ever get exasperated with your child (surely not!) – imagine having twenty odd other adolescents in your kitchen at the same time.
- The lure of 'normality' is strong. There is a huge emotional premium from being told your child is able enough to cope into the 'mainstream'
- Parents need to take a step back and see the bigger picture for their academically able autistic children. Nobody else in 'the system' has a holistic brief for their child.
- We *know* our children are prone to depression in adolescence and early adulthood.
- We *know* that chronic stress can bring on depression.
- We *know* that mainstream secondary schooling can engender chronic stress in many children with AS.
- A swathe of anecdotal evidence points to autistic adolescents having esteem destroying experiences in mainstream secondary schools -

despite the best efforts of the many good people who try to help them while they are there.

- There **would,** therefore, seem a transmission mechanism between the current modus operandi of mainstream secondary schools and the mental health problems of adolescents with AS.

- We **have** to focus on the **prevention** of Depression because there is no effective curative system for adolescents. Anti-depressant Drugs are increasingly viewed as inappropriate for young people, and there is minimal mental health provision for adolescents on both sides of the Irish sea.

- No child should enter adolescence with a disability and exit adolescence with a disability *AND* mental health problems because of the inflexibility of educational provision.

- Insisting that children with AS are exposed full-frontal to institutions that may damage their mental health impinges on a fundamental human right. The real choice is between a modest investment from the education budget early on, or a much greater investment from the mental health budget later on.

- The notion of '*Inclusion'* is often poorly defined, embraced by those who have finite budgets to manage, and is at odds with the core function of mainstream secondary schools. It is a woolly logic that extrapolates from what might be right for disability in general, to what is right for all autistic adolescents.

- Because children with AS come across as 'more able' than the majority of children with intellectual disabilities there is a tendency to see it as a 'mild' handicap. In adolescence it is anything but that. It is precisely their 'near- normalness' that makes them targets for daily derision and 'internal exclusion'. Far from *including* them we are giving them intensive doses of daily exclusion courtesy of their peers. They are not 'off-limits' for predators – as are children with more overt disabilities. They are at the head of the queue for all the insensitivity a teenage mind can muster. Whatever it says in the schools anti-bullying policy, if your child has AS they **will** be teased and bullied in a mainstream school. All a school can attempt to do is minimise the incidence and severity of the bullying.

- Adolescence is a defining time for everybody – but this is especially the case for a person with AS. The psychological battering they get in secondary school can stay with them for a lifetime.

- Mainstream secondary schools are institutionally **exclusive**. They are obliged to pursue a narrow agenda that often ill suits the long-term needs of many autistic students. In England the manic focus on school league tables has made this situation worse.

- Given the number of 'triggers' inherent in a mainstream school, the learning environment is often at odds with the needs of the autistic student. If the object of the exercise is to have a child learn in the most *effective* environment then the logic of a mainstream placement is further in doubt. Stress inhibits effective learning.

- School at secondary level involves stretching many autistic children's social, executive and sensory capacity to the limit. Stress levels maintained at this point for months on end may undermine immune systems. Chronic stress makes people unwell.

- For the most academically gifted of children with AS a mainstream placement *may* still be the best option. A degree in Engineering or Computing is life enhancing **if** it can be acquired at a reasonable cost. Teaching in the core subjects that underpin these disciplines is not easy to replicate outside the mainstream. And there **is** a huge premium to be had from securing a degree and a prestigious job. It certainly enhances prospects with the opposite sex! But there *are* risks and, whilst these are less quantifiable than the benefits, they have to be factored in. What is the point of getting a degree but ending up unable to use it because of mental health problems or minimal social skills.

- For the many children with AS whose 'Swiss-cheese' portfolio does *not* contain numeracy as a strength, the balance of costs and benefits shifts even more against a full-time mainstream placement. Virtually all subjects in a secondary school require proficiency in numbers; it is implicitly assumed in all the subject schemes of work that age-appropriate numerical ability exists. If a child cannot comply with this expectation they will not achieve examination grades that will open any doors. In which case a really big question mark must hang over the entire exercise. A daily diet of relative *failure* in **every** aspect of school life – academic subjects, socially, practical subjects, sporting activities, artistic pursuits, **cannot** be good for a child.

- As adolescence kicks in, there will be a growing awareness of these failings and a growing frustration with them. To the extent a child is unaware of their deficiencies their peers – and the odd insensitive teacher – will soon rectify that blissful ignorance.

- There is a **trade-off** between time spent on achieving paper qualifications and time available to develop social/life/mental health/PN skills. These crucial skills are unlikely to be picked up incidentally.

- Adolescents with AS require a markedly different curriculum. It is a curriculum that is **not** being provided for the majority of children with AS in mainstream schools in these islands.

- Some schools will view the effort involved in designing a *truly* individualised curriculum more as a nuisance than an opportunity. What currently appears on paper as an IEP is rarely translated into reality.

- Recent initiatives (England) on 'individualised education ' will change nothing whilst the core function of a school remains as narrow as it is, and fear of failure (judged by *very* narrow criteria) is the driving force.

- Finding paid employment can confer status and improve quality of life. But interviews will be problematic. Surrendering benefits will cause anxiety. Many adults with AS end up with a patchy and stressful employment record. And bullying at work – and college - is a common enough problem.

- Work placement needs to be managed and supported. People with AS should not be left to sink or swim just because they reach the age of 18.

- We need to be giving equal status to the strengths of each child, and to be imaginative in nurturing their passions. To focus purely on 'fixing' them and exam preparation is tantamount to child abuse.

- We need to latch onto the whole person at the age of 12 and take them on an individualised journey that sees school as a resource to be used for the benefit of the child.

- Provision should be flexible and sensitive. Slavish adherence to a *national* curriculum does not constitute inclusion.

- If in doubt keep 'em out.

- Children of secondary school age with AS need a dedicated Personal **Tutor/Life Coach** to effect this individualised journey. This may be a parent or a person appointed to the role.

- Parents should have a *Plan B* in mind in case their local mainstream secondary school cannot or will not deliver a programme that, in their view, minimises stress and maximises potential.

- Fostering self-esteem delivers a happier and more sustainable outcome than relentless interventions that seek to 'fix' the child.

- People with AS will *always* have a comparative disadvantage *'socially'*; It is sufficient to seek their collaboration on the elimination of traits that polite society would deem as unacceptable.

- Sleep, exercise, and laughter are huge factors in the healing process

He will be 18 this November. I have an old suitcase containing assorted memorabilia to hand to him. One of the items is a diary I kept for the first 12 months of his life. It was all about what he was up to, and my hopes for his future. I don't remember exactly what I wrote – all will be revealed soon enough - but I do know I couldn't be prouder of the way he has turned out.

Bibliography

The Report of the Task force on Autism. Dept of Ed.and Science. (Ireland)

Incorporating Social Goals in the Classroom' by Rebecca Moyes -'

Inclusion and Autism: Is it working? by Barnard Prior and Potter NAS

Hansard

Access and Inclusion for children with Autistic Spectrum Disorders: Matthew Hemondshalgh and Christine Breakey

Trevor Trevor: Diane Twachtmann-Cullen

Making Friends: Andrew Matthews

Autism: Preparing for Adulthood: Patricia Howlin

Asperger's Syndrome – A guide for parents and professionals'
: Tony Attwood

AS in Adolescence ed by Liane Holliday Willey

The Curious Incident of the Dog in the Night-time: Mark Haddon

Printed in the United Kingdom
by Lightning Source UK Ltd.
114486UKS00001B/385-462